This is a continuation in the series of publications produced by the Center for Advanced Concepts and Technology (ACT), which was created as a "skunk works" with funding provided by the CCRP under the auspices of the Assistant Secretary of Defense (NII). This program has demonstrated the importance of having a research program focused on the national security implications of the Information Age. It develops the theoretical foundations to provide DoD with information superiority and highlights the importance of active outreach and dissemination initiatives designed to acquaint senior military personnel and civilians with these emerging issues. The CCRP Publication Series is a key element of this effort.

Check our Web site for the latest CCRP activities and publications.

www.dodccrp.org

DoD Command and Control Research Program

Assistant Secretary of Defense (NII)
&
Chief Information Officer
Dr. Linton Wells, II (Acting)

Principal Deputy Assistant Secretary of Defense (NII)
Dr. Linton Wells, II

Special Assistant to the ASD(NII)
&
Director of Research
Dr. David S. Alberts

Library of Congress Cataloging-in-Publication Data

Atkinson, Simon, 1969-
The agile organization : from informal networks to complex effects and agility / Simon Reay Atkinson, James Moffat.
    p. cm. -- (Information age transformation series)
  Includes bibliographical references and index.
  ISBN 1-893723-16-X (alk. paper)
1. Organizational change. 2. Organizational effectiveness. 3. Business networks. I. Moffat, James, 1948- II. Title. III. Series.
Cover and illustrations by Joseph Lewis
HD58.8.A89 2005
658.4'06--dc22

                                                    2005013433

July 2005

Information Age Transformation Series

THE AGILE ORGANIZATION

FROM INFORMAL NETWORKS TO COMPLEX EFFECTS AND AGILITY

SIMON REAY ATKINSON

JAMES MOFFAT

Simon Reay Atkinson

This book is dedicated to my wife Susie
and my son Samuel John-Reay:
to a better future for our children.

James Moffat

This book is dedicated to my wife Jacqueline
and my daughters Louise and Katherine.

Both authors would like to acknowledge the debt they owe to loyal, ever constructively critical, friends in the U.S. Department of Defense, other agencies, and academia. These professional American military and civil servants, academics, and scientists from many different backgrounds, having suffered from 9/11 and more recent events, continue to believe in the spirit that made America great and which, despite many setbacks, mistakes, and adversity, has so much to offer the world in the future.

"No man is an island, entire of itself; every man is a piece of the continent, a part of the main; if a clod be washed away by the sea, Europe is the less, as well as if a promontory were, as well as if a manor of thy friends or of thine own were; any man's death diminishes me, because I am involved in mankind; and therefore never send to know for whom the bell tolls; it tolls for thee."

John Donne
(1572-1631)

TABLE OF CONTENTS

LIST OF FIGURES

PHOTOGRAPHY CREDITS

FOREWORD

A gility is the gold standard for Information Age militaries. Facing uncertain futures and new sets of threats in a complex, dynamic, and challenging security environment, militaries around the world are transforming themselves, becoming more information-enabled and network-centric.

Command and control is at the heart of these transformations. Traditional approaches to command and control are being questioned, as new approaches are being explored. Perhaps the most significant aspect of this nascent revolution in how militaries organize, operate, and think about themselves and their adversaries is the change in the criteria for success. Traditional militaries and military analysis focus squarely on mission effectiveness for a set of selected missions (approved planning scenarios). Information Age militaries searching for a way to deal with the complexities, uncertainties, and risks associated with the 21st century security environment are discovering the virtues of agility, not only as a core competency in operations, but as a value metric for policy and investment decisions.

Agility has been a theme in CCRP publications for more than a decade. In *Command Arrangements* (1995), it was noted that a lack of agility threatened mission success. In *Information Age*

Transformation (2002), agility was defined as a key characteristic of an Information Age organization "of paramount importance in an uncertain world," "a characteristic to be sought even at the sacrifice of seeking to perfect capabilities associated with specific missions or tasks" (page 82).

Information Age Transformation also defined the attributes of agility as including responsiveness, robustness, innovativeness, flexibility, and adaptability (page 83). *Power to the Edge* (2003) devoted an entire chapter to agility, and added the attribute resiliency, which was formerly included as a sense of robustness, the ability to maintain performance in the face of degradation (pages 123-127).

Agility is related to the ability to conduct network-centric operations (NCO) and is associated with Power to the Edge principles. A robustly networked force is, by virtue of its increased connectedness, more agile. An improved information position clearly enables agility, while the concept of speed of command that is associated with a network-centric force is closely related to the responsiveness attribute of agility. On the other hand, collaboration, part of the tenets of NCW, may or may not result in increased agility. It depends upon the skills and experience of the participants, the nature of the situation, and the quality of the collaborative environment. Because collaborative processes offer some real benefits, in and of themselves, understanding how to accomplish them in ways that result in more rather than less agility is important. Self-synchronization, an important aspect of network-centric operations, is related to a number of the attributes of agility.

Power to the Edge principles, particularly those that involve increasing the ability of the edge to understand and act, are related to agility. In fact, *Power to the Edge* states that "edge organizations have the attributes to be agile. This is because agility requires that available information is combined in new ways, that a variety of perspectives are brought to bear, and that assets can be employed differently to meet the needs of a variety of situations" (page 217).

The agility of an enterprise is a function of how it is organized and more specifically, a function of its approach to command and control. Approaches to command and control and to the resulting organization differ significantly with respect to the agility they offer or, perhaps more to the point, with the constraints that are placed on agility, specifically constraints on information sharing, interactions, and constraints on the way assets can be employed.

This book, *The Agile Organization*, explores the nature and behaviors of different kinds of networked enterprises and their implications for military organizations. The authors take us on a conceptual journey across the landscape that is Complexity. They offer us valuable insights into systems, networks, organizations, and, of course, into the nature of command and control. Atkinson and Moffat have taken a number of theories and concepts articulated and discussed in the CCRP Publication Series, improved and built upon them, and have make a significant contribution to the field. They have also afforded us a rare opportunity to view the challenges we face through a different lens.

This book is also an indicant of the growing recognition that new organizational forms and approaches to command and control are needed to meet the security challenges of the 21st century. We look forward to working with colleagues from around the world to better understand the nature of agility and agile organizations.

Dr. David S. Alberts
Washington, DC
May 2005

CHAPTER 1

STOP THE WORLD,
I WANT TO GET OFF!

About a thousand years ago, the Moffat clan were farmers in southwest Scotland where the River Annan runs from the Southern Uplands down into the Solway Firth. The modern town of Moffat still stands just south of there—a pretty tourist sort of a place, with a large statue of a ram in the main street to remind us all of its agricultural roots. In those former times, the clans were isolated and disconnected from each other, yet internally very closely tied together. Travel across land was difficult; without roads, only the extremities of war against the common enemy England brought them together. The Atkinson clan came from the Eastern borderlands of England and Scotland, from Cumberland and the South Tyne near where it flows past Alston, the highest market town in England, to the Forth—across the "debatable lands" between Scotland and England that for centuries was the home of the "Reivers"—and from Norse stock; sharing both a Tartan and the Northumberland pipes. The Moffats and Atkinsons are still farmers today, but like the Scottish (and British migrants, trav-

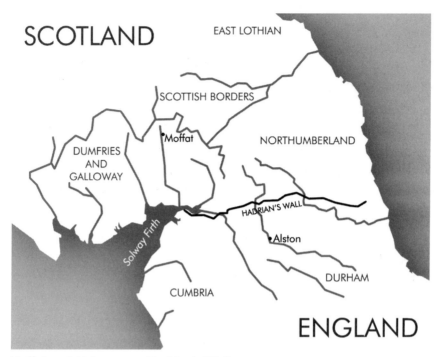

Moffat and Alston, near Hadrian's Wall

ellers, scientists, diplomats, engineers, sailors and) soldiers they became, their clans have travelled "far way"—to the Americas, Australasia, Africa, and Asia. The names of their farms, such as Gladstone-Boreland and High Dryburn, are still rooted (often fortified) and so connected back to the history of the land. But gradually over the centuries, as technology and society have evolved, links have been made that now knit together our connected modern society with its past, its present, and so its future. The two clans remain connected, but not so much by geography and circumstance as history and a shared understanding of each other and a common trust in the future.

Networks have thus always been with us; they are not new, and neither is Complexity or the forms, patterns, and shapes that emerge from its constructs to provide meaning, if not understanding, to the many interlinked and connected issues that confront us today. Things have changed, of course, and they continue to do so. Key to the way things have changed, even in the last 10 years, has been our ability to connect nodes and peoples across the globe to create effects, some new, in different parts of the world remotely, and in complex ways never before possible. This connectedness has bypassed the older, more rule-based structures and placed a means of creating effects within new groupings and organizations. These organizations have behaved in different and often threatening ways that have undermined or simply bypassed the old, less agile systems, based more normatively upon rules and consensus. States, companies, and organizations unable to adapt agilely to the new ways, means, and methods of working have succumbed. Security, the old preserve of the state, is often now provided privately within gated communities and/or by criminal organizations whose networks criss-cross more effectively the North-South divide and the Third World than any state-sponsored or derived organizations, such as the U.N. or NGOs.

In the spring of 2003, Professor Jim Moffat and Commander Simon Reay Atkinson came together at a Ministry of Defence Conference on Network Connected this and Enabled Capability that and, between the sessions, determined that something was missing. That, while many people were there for good reasons, their core understanding of the subject, its complexity, breadth, and indeed its mystery were not being deepened, but obfuscated in the urgency of the moment and by the pressures of a system that requires instant understanding and solutions, now; and that in our processes and hunt for the instant we are in danger of forgetting our past and so misinterpreting our future.

This book endeavours to explore this terrain, to look at Complexity, Networks, and Formal Organizations from a British military and policy making perspective. It does not attempt to be a new book on management or the social sciences, although clearly there are lessons that may be derived by both disciplines. Neither does it attempt to advocate an alternative philosophy for international relations or a new doctrine for the military. Instead, it attempts to place the military in context so that it can better understand itself, the complex adaptive world it faces, the ways and means it may wish to aggregate, and how it is to be commanded and so controlled in a way in which we might confront our enemies of today and tomorrow adaptively, agilely, and with confidence. We start, in chapters 2, 3, and 4, by introducing the ideas of Complexity, Complex Adaptive Systems (CAS), and complex networks of interaction. Some real examples of how such informal networks are created that complement the institutional structures are discussed. In chapters 5 and 6, we introduce the ideas of the creation of effects and agility. Finally, these are brought together in chapter 7. We will show at each chapter heading how these ideas evolve under the series of headings:

Complexity ➡ Networks ➡ Effects ➡ Agility

GLOBALIZATION

Nature abhors a vacuum[1] and into the "chaos" of failing states and communities, new structures formed—in many regards going back in time to man's earliest days as he learned to aggregate and communicate with others. These new structures provided basic requirements and replaced the failing and cor-

---

[1] Attributed to Aristotle (384-322 B.C.) as applied subsequently by the American Philosopher, Henry David Thoreau (1817-1862).

rupted organs of an increasingly moribund and ineffective state system—at least in many developing countries—with edifices of security and survival in which people could trust and believe. We may not have liked the fact that these edifices provided security through the barrel of a gun and their economies were based on crime, but many were tolerated through the logic of "the enemy of my enemy is my friend." That was until 9/11 and indeed shortly beforehand—in Sierra-Leone, for example—where the new nature of international crime became more and more threatening to our peace.

Globalization has changed that safe—if false—perception we had of the world in the late 20th century. Globalization means that no state can remain an island; we are in fact connected and interconnected with each other in ways never previously thought possible. The Afghan poppy grower exporting his crop to your streets is as connected with our markets, our national health system, police, customs, and excise—your taxes in fact—as is your milkman. He has very different overheads, perhaps, but his output directly contributes to our outcomes. The immigrant fleeing from a non-applicable state, for whatever reason, connects to us—via the courts or illegal employers—and through the same state systems back to the place from which he came. We cannot address either drugs or migration in isolation to demand—the demand on our streets for opiates or the demand of migrants for a better life. Through the explicit interactivity of globalization we are connected, and not just for good. We are talking here about many complex and highly adaptive systems, themselves forming a system of systems or networks of networks. And, like any Complex Adaptive System, they cannot be controlled or ruled: a CAS will simply find ways of working around the rules if the context in which it formed remains viable. Drugs and migrants will still get through, despite the rules.

The basis of these new systems of working and aggregating is that they are based upon very simple trusts—not rules—as often as not, basic trusts regarding survival, of earning one's daily bread one day, and waking up to earn it the next. These are simple things to you and I, who enjoy living in societies within which law and order are still maintained, but they are vastly different for the young boy from Sierra-Leone who has watched his parents murdered and who has been forced, through a combination of drugs and brutality, to become a child soldier for the local warlord—and whose survival now rests in his ability to kill. The boy from Sierra-Leone makes a choice, based upon his immediate need for survival and the organizations to which he feels sufficiently connected to, to trust. We might not like it and the boy is not likely to live long, but he has made a logical choice. The organizations such people join are not the state or its police or security organs, but the criminal networks that have evolved to fill the vacuum of law and order, wherever they find it. A recent well-organized police action on the south coast of England involved the removal of a local and highly influential (well-connected) drug-baron. The operation went well and the drug-baron was arrested. Days, not even weeks or months later, the criminal networks had reformed themselves; supply had hardly been interrupted.

Disaggregated as they are and based upon trusts within and across their boundaries—in order to satisfy often simple requirements, such as demand—these networks are highly agile and adaptive. Removing one well-connected hub, or cluster, from within one cell, simply enables new connections to form. The fundamental context in which these networks emerged in the first place—to satisfy a need—has not changed. And the networks are sufficiently concentrated and overlapping for the removal of one hub to make only a transient difference to the whole.

IDEALISM AND REALISM, TRUST AND RULES

The nature of the way people aggregate and the trusts and rules they form within these groups and between others are fundamental to our way of thinking and working. They form the underlying truths of the ways different communities and groups work together and with others and, over time, they define the philosophy by which a group is understood. Some philosophers of the 20th century considered two different forms of aggregation. *Idealism* set store by the creation of rules by which people could live in peace, and that led to the creation of the League of Nations and subsequently to the United Nations. *Realism* denied the premise upon which idealists based their claims and looked instead to power politics in a bipolar world, defined then by the West and the U.S. and the East and Communism. They argued that states were rational players and, beyond rules, they would work and fight for their own survival, based upon the best interests of the state—not a remote nirvana incumbent upon idealized, international (unenforceable) rules of behavior. The enemy of my enemy is my friend. Our supposition, and one that emerges from this book, is that it is false to divide the ideals by which people define their lives from the rules they use to live them by. Essentially, the tension is not between *Idealism* and *Realism* but between *trusts* and *rules*.

Networks are defined by the trusts that bind and so define them, but these same networks, at certain moments in time and space, need more formal organizations to protect and safeguard them through agreed rules of behavior and conduct. For example, a very networked organization working autonomously and asynchronously relies upon formal organizations, based upon rules, by which its members are paid each month, accounts are settled, and bills raised. For the network to work and so transfer power to and from its edge efficiently and effectively, it relies on some form of rule-based power source. This rule-based formal organization may not be at its center but will be a part of the hub or cluster about which the network is formed. If the network is to be effective—to create effects—it needs a source of power from which its nodes can exercise power. This organization needs to have formal arrangements, or rules, agreed upon between the different members (nodes, hubs/clusters). To work effectively, the rules by which the formal organization operates need to be based upon the trusts that define the network and the way it aggregates.

Returning to the philosophical division between Realism and Idealism, a network is formed from the trusts or beliefs of its base organization—the reality it confronts; whereas formal organizations are defined by the rules necessary to preserve and protect the beliefs of the network—the ideals by which the network lives. Essentially, Realists need Idealists, and vice versa. Neither can exist effectively without the other and the tension that exists between the two has more to do with a requirement for the rules, by which the organization lives, to reflect the trusts that define it. There are many examples of organizations where the rules by which they are expected to live have parted company from the trusts that define them. The Sierra-Leone boy does not play by the rules of law and order, for which the conditions have long since disappeared. He trusts in what he sees and has to believe in, and his rules of conduct are defined by the trusts and confidences of his group. If he breaks these rules, he knows the consequences; whereas, if he breaks the rules of the state and happens to be caught, he knows he will survive, provided he does not breach the trusts of his group. The only way the state can change this "reality" is by changing the conditions or ideals by which these networks form in the first place—so that they form around and not in antipathy to the formal organizations and rules of the state.

POST-MODERNISM AND POST-BELIEF

In this regard, too, the philosophy of Post-Modernism—that denies any single truth or belief—may also be reflected in our understanding of organizations and how they form and aggregate. The networks we consider are held together by certain trusts in which individuals believe. These trusts and beliefs are often different from those that define others and it is these that make the group or organization "different." Where these different organizations come into contact and/or overlap, certain rules of conduct are necessary to define how they work together if conflict is to be avoided. These rules need to reflect the underlying beliefs and truths by which the different organizations exist. In this regard, the Peace of Westphalia—much heralded as being the basis from which three essential constructs of the modern (Western) world emerged: The State (and the division of state and politics from religion); International Law; and Western Laws of War (and Peace)—was actually more about a sectarian settlement between Protestants from the north of Europe and Catholics from the south. It enabled both different means of aggregation and organization to coexist peaceably after years of irresolvable conflict. It also released two very different philosophies: one, to the north, essentially international and outward-looking and the other, in the south, more inward-looking, based upon rules to ensure the peace of central Europe.

Modernism needs also to be looked at in relation to its derivation in terms of "Modern History"—generally accepted to have begun on the invasion of Egypt (and the old world) by France and Napoleon in 1798 and its ejection by Britain and Nelson in the same year. Post-Modernism was therefore about both a rejection of modern, and thereby Western, constructs and beliefs, as it was a reflection that there are many different ways, or truths, by which peoples and organizations define themselves. Taken to its extreme, as perhaps identified by philosophers such as Jacques Derrida, Post-Modernism claimed "that meaning—or belief—was subject to limitless interpretation so that everything could be made to mean anything."[2] This perhaps is not so much *Post-Modernism* as *Post-Belief*. The difficulty many modern societies face is that, once the beliefs or trusts are removed, the way they define themselves and the rules by which they live no longer have meaning. In a network sense, the trusts that defined the network and so the rules by which it organized have been removed. The network may continue but it no longer is capable of exercising power and effectiveness and its rules no longer reflect its beliefs or truths. Ultimately, it can no longer be trusted—a vacuum has formed.

The way we aggregate therefore defines our trusts and so our beliefs and thereby the rules by which we are prepared to live and interpret our lives. European society, post World War II and the Cold War, may be defined more as being Post-Belief than Post-Modern. The beliefs upon which European society

---

[2] Robin Young, writing in the The Times on the death of Jacques Derrida, Monday October 11 2004: "This may mean something or not."

formed have been replaced by new rules—the Peace of Europe—constructed after World War II, through the European Steel and Coal Pact, to prevent France and Germany from ever again going to war. European nations have pooled their trusts into a single belief in peace and the avoidance of conflict through the denial of any one single predominant belief. To a great extent, the experiment has worked, but the experiment may also be testing the peripheral regions (the new as opposed to old Europe) in the tension between newly won democratic forms of aggregation and a bureaucratic, apolitical, a-belief, and non-elected rule from Brussels, as opposed to Moscow. From a network perspective, it is as if we have used rules to define our trusts—representation without taxation. The U.S. political system continues to be based upon beliefs: belief in religion, President, God, and Country. They also believe (as many in Europe do) in the threat posed by Jihad and extremist Islam. And Jihadists, similarly, believe that they are in violent and continuing Jihad with the West—not just the U.S.—and that their form of aggregation under Islam and through Umah (the Muslim "Nation") is the only way. However, in a Post-Belief society no longer aggregated along common trusts, it is likely to prove more difficult to believe in another's beliefs, particularly if these beliefs threaten the very foundation upon which one's own peace has been constructed. This returns to the way in which we aggregate and how networks and formal organizations evolve and form to reflect the many different truths that confront us. The underlying truth about networks, based upon trusts, and formal organizations, constructed about rules, is that they both need each other if trusts are to be maintained and laws upheld. It also reflects the need for different organizations, at certain times and places, to determine new ways of working together if they are not to be in perpetual conflict.

NETWORKS AND ORGANIZATIONS IN PARTNERSHIP

This book is not about challenging philosophers, although some of the conclusions we draw may cause them to think again; it is about explaining the complex phenomena concerning the way we aggregate in terms that we may understand. The way we aggregate defines who we are, what we do, and how successful (or not) we become. We are all members of many different networks—family, clans, churches, associations, schools, and so on—and we are also members of formal organizations, such as banks, companies, regiments, ships, and clubs at the same time. And within the networks we are a part of, there are formal organizations, and within the formal organizations that we join, there are networks. The two exist in partnership. Over time, they also define us as we define them so that the inherent philosophies of the networks and formal organizations to which we belong reflect the trusts and rules by which we live our lives. If we want to understand the way in which we see the world, we need to understand the prism through which our views are constructed. What we see we may not like, but the way in which we aggregate ourselves is fundamental to the way in which we are seen by others and express ourselves to them. As Sun Tzu observed, if you "know your enemy and know yourself, then you will not be endangered in a hundred battles." It is through this knowing of oneself and how one's own forms are aggregated that one can understand one's own weaknesses and strengths, and so what is threatening, or not, to one's enemy. Thus, if we can understand networks and how they operate, aggregate, and perform—their fears and desires—we can also understand how others perform, and so know what to do and what not to do.

WHAT WORKS

In the military, too, we have to maintain certain immutable trusts and beliefs in each other and, unfashionably, in God, Queen, and Country. We do so because these are the beliefs that, when combined with our trusts in our fellow man, troop, platoon, ship, company, squadron, or regiment, enable us to go out and fight, kill, and, if necessary, die. We do not lead on the basis of rules but on trusts and beliefs in each other foremost, and then the cascading sense of belief that defines us as soldiers, sailors, and airmen. Similarly, we do not fight as a formal organization, a ship, or a regiment, although that is what we are known by in the media and to the rest of the world. We fight as networked sailors or soldiers in our platoons, troops, and divisions amongst people we trust and do not want to let down. It is a simple code, when all is said and done, established over the years and based on trusts and beliefs in each other foremost, and then the wider organizations to which we belong. We have based ourselves upon military perceptions and examples of how different forms of aggregation have worked or may be made to work. We take this analysis from a scientific understanding of Complexity, Networks, and Organizations, and apply them in contemporary settings that may be understood by military policy makers.

In our initial discussions, we both also agreed that we needed a book that was based upon good rhetoric, not just good math; rhetoric that took complicated subjects and their mathematical derivations and then explained them in a way that may more readily be understood and read by those from a wider community. For, underlying the theory of Complexity and Networks is not mathematics, science, and technology, but people—the way we work and aggregate ourselves.

THE FUTURE INTO WHICH WE GAZE

The world in the 21st century looks much more threatening than it did at the end of the Second World War. But, at the same time, we are seeing new and complex patterns emerge with historical resonance in the Balkans, Africa, Asia, and Europe. New means of aggregation are forming to occupy the spaces created by the collapse of the Soviet Union, and the ways they are forming reflect the contexts in which people find themselves. Globalization and the explosion in information technologies are forming linkages and connections—for both good and bad—that we cannot ignore and that we cannot prevent from forming. We can no longer stand back and ignore the networks, because they impact upon our way of life or our values; they are now connected directly to us.

In the past, the Ministry of Defence considered Warning Time for a conventional state-on-state war to be comprised of Decision Time, Readiness, Preparation and Training Time, and Deployment Time. In some instances, this Warning Time might be as long as 10 years, in others months. And for each we predicated different scales of warfare with which we may be likely to fight: large, medium, or small. We also defined Threat to be equal to our enemies' capability, capacity,[3] and intent or will. Clearly our Warning Time must also be some function of the Threat, and vice versa. If we consider what happened on 9/11, Warning Time for various reasons was effectively zero. In other words, the threat was pervasive and already there—the only way the U.S. could have countered the attacks at that moment was to have shot the planes down. To do so, they

---

[3] Capacity is not part of the traditional "Threat" equation, but it may be considered a network value in terms of connectivity, breadth, and depth.

Satellite photography of New York and the Pentagon on the day after the 9/11 attacks

would have required aircraft on station, ready and armed, beyond the airspace of New York and with the necessary authority to engage at the instant that the aircraft came within range. Essentially, in a highly connected world, peace and war are perpetually joined—our peace is connected to another's war, just as another's peace is connected to our war. In such a networked environment, where the enemy combines his capacity and will/intent with our capabilities (aircraft, technologies, IT, rules, and media) against us, then we will have little or no Warning Time.

The revolution that occurred on 9/11 also swept away the old certainties by which war was joined historically and that defined peace as the cessation of war. It left our policy makers with a grim choice. If they cannot engage with the other and prevent his networks from forming in hostility to our own val-

The future into which we gaze

ues and ways of working, before the event, or if it is already too late, then we are left only with pre-emption, with all that that implies. If we consider both 9/11 and the tragedy at Beslan, once the terrorists had boarded the aircraft or entered the school, it was too late. The only way in which the tragedies could have been avoided was to have stopped them from being committed in the first place. Given time, prevention might work; in other cases, one is left only with pre-emption. And for pre-emption to work, one needs intelligence with the fidelity and agility to accurately target the threat. Even with the right intelligence, one still needs decisionmakers with the courage, understanding, and leadership to make difficult decisions. They will not win praise either way—there is no credit for preventing something that did not happen.

In coalitions in particular, but alliances too, it is the exchange of trusts between different military organizations that determines their effectiveness. If I do not trust you to fight with me, then I will have to organize for you to fight alongside me in a demarcated fashion that avoids fratricide. In the First Gulf War, Allies were demarcated from each other because they did not have the identification systems to avoid blue-on-blue fratricide and, put simply, did not have the confidence and trusts to fight together. In the Second Gulf War, British, American, and Australian forces fought under and with each other in ways that were at least interoperable, and at times integrated. They were seamless to an outsider, with decisions being made by Americans and carried out by Britons, and vice versa.

This part of the new battlespace cannot be ruled or controlled: it can only be commanded, based upon the trusts and shared beliefs of coalition forces. And the effectiveness of these organizations is based, in part—if not in full—on the degree of integration they achieve. And this degree, in turn, is based upon the trusts individual soldiers, sailors, and airmen, from different countries and organizations, have in each other to do the right thing. These are network structures, not ruled formal organizations, and as such, whilst they can be assisted techno-logically, they are based upon shared cultural understandings and beliefs. They are more about people than systems or tech-nologies. And these means of aggregation, of sharing and transferring trusts, define not simply how we look and behave, but also how we are commanded and controlled.

The challenge to the military is not so much to make its fight-ing structures more networkable, since they are inherently so already, but to ensure that the way forces are commanded and controlled, and policies are formed, are coherent and similarly adaptive and agile to the forces they command. Put simply, such complex systems cannot be controlled, and to attempt to do so would be to deny the network its fidelity, agility, and trusts to do the right thing. They can, however, be influenced, bounded, and placed within an appropriate context.

CHAPTER 2

COMPLEXITY: NEW INSIGHTS INTO SYSTEMS AND NETWORKS

Complexity ➡

In this and the following two chapters, we introduce the notions of Complexity, Complex Adaptive Systems, and complex networks of interaction together with some real examples. These form the foundation for the introduction of the ideas of effects and agility in chapters 5 and 6.

Globalization, in the terms set out in this work, is about connectedness between, across, above, below, and through pre-existing political, religious, economic, thematic, and geographic or security boundaries. Whereas previously it was possible to separate political and religious boundaries behind largely geographic and historically defined frontiers, this is no longer possible. Thus, Western Europe and Russia, after the final fall of Constantinople and the completion of the Spanish Reconquista, could be defined as Christian; the Middle East, East Africa, Central Asia and Southeast Asia as

Muslim. This began to be distorted in the 19th century with the mass migrations from Europe to the New World, and the U.S., Australia, Canada, and Argentina in particular. But, with the exception of the westward migration of the Jews from Russia to Germany, Britain, and the U.S., this migration was mostly Caucasian and "Christian."

The 20th century, in broad terms, witnessed a clash of ideals between Germany, Britain, and France for control of central Europe and then between Communism, Fascism, and Capitalism—all essentially European ideals, exported to the rest of the world. After 1914, the mass "economic" migration that had defined the 19th century ceased, held behind an isolationist U.S. and barriers to trade erected by the British Empire after 1919. Exhaustion after WWI and stagnation in the U.K., the U.S., and France, collapse in Germany, and revolution in Russia all conspired to isolate each from the other—exacerbated by tariffs/barriers to trade, isolationism, and Britain's return to the Gold Standard.[4] The interaction of ideas and ideals that had so defined the 19th century through trade, industry, migration, and colonialization ceased.

The pax or peace of the 19th century—constructed largely by Britain and other colonial powers for the exchange of peace (law and order) and security for goods and labor—broke down. The essential interactions that enabled the pax to exist—the three-way exchange of capital (migration provides a form of capital exchange in its own right[5]), people (including ideas and

---

[4] Instigated by Churchill.

[5] Migration in the 19th century was by no means one way. Migrants went to the U.S. and sometimes returned to their original homes having made their fortunes. Most importantly, migrants sent money back to their families, providing both a source of income and a reduced burden on them.

ideals), and trade (including law, order, property, security, and commerce)—stopped in its tracks.

After WWII, interaction was minimized and the world was even more isolated behind the walls of both the Soviet Union and the West—the shared purpose of the new peace, defined by Lord Ismay (NATO's first Secretary General), was "to keep the Russians out, the Americans in, and the Germans down." Behind these mutually supporting walls (the Soviet Union wanted to keep Germany down, for which it was prepared to accept America in, at the price of Russia being out), traditional migration routes (except for a handful of defectors on both sides) almost stopped and, as the European empires collapsed, the older colonial interactions also ceased.

The Cold War essentially stopped the global interactions that had defined the more complex world that had existed between the 16th and 19th centuries in their tracks, confining exchanges, interactions, and the peace along black and white lines. After 1989, the simplistic definition of identity by differentiating and consolidating one side by "what it is not" (for example, communist or capitalist, West or East) rather than "what it is" was no longer possible.[6]

> Today, the emphasis has been shifted to the actors and issues: human rights, migration, ethnic conflict, small-arms flows, dislocations and disparities generated by economic globalization, intensified information flows, environmental and immunological concerns, religious

---

[6] The Turkish Cypriot psychoanalyst Vamik Volkan addresses this issue in his book: *The Need to have Enemies and Allies.*

movements and global criminal networks. These can all transcend, disrupt, and bypass state interests.[7]

It is this newly emerging complexity of new connections and re-established old connections that will define our future—who we are to become as much as who we are. Globalization therefore poses many challenges to the way we aggregate, how we see ourselves, and so see the opportunities and threats that will confront us in the 21st century. In some regards, they will be similar to those that existed before the 20th century and in others very different. Historically, the 20th century may be seen as the exception and not the norm of man's means of aggregating with his fellow man. We examine these new transnational challenges to our security from the viewpoint of Complexity and the new types of aggregation that will emerge to address them.

Returning to Dr. Sayigh:

> the apparent anarchy of globalization and inchoate nature of some of its social and political consequences reveals two forms of an emerging organized response. One is a wide and evolving variety of networks that may spread across state and non-state sectors and may encompass both legal and illegal groups and activities. In some potentially threatening cases, these networks may apply modern technological expertise (from nuclear, biological, chemical [NBC] capabilities to the Internet) against populations, critical infrastructure, or IT-based systems and cause devastation. The other

---

[7] Dr. Yezid Sayigh, writing in: "The Cambridge Security," Seminar Record. 30-31 July 2004. p. 11.

response is a reassertion of state power and centralization.[8]

Global politics, global economics, and global security are therefore connected in many different and complex forms—some networked and others along more hierarchical or state lines. To understand these new forms of global aggregation (or globalization), we need to understand the complex interactions that define them and so define "complexity."

We begin our journey with the thought that we tend to think about problems and issues in terms of models and metaphors that are familiar. In many cases, these models and metaphors are generated by our scientific understanding of how nature works. Intuitively, we understand that what drives natural systems can and must also apply to us as part of nature. For example, it is commonplace to read in a newspaper about the "momentum" of a political party, the "evolution" of an idea, or a "quantum leap" in our understanding (although this depends to some extent on the quality of your newspaper of choice). What is new is that these fundamental metaphors are changing, and a new language is emerging that allows us to think about complexity—and that applies to the complexity of modern life and society.

Back in the clockwork Newtonian universe, we thought we understood what was going on: "God said let Newton be and all was light." Newton made two bold hypotheses: firstly that what we understood locally (in or around the earth's gravity in his case) applied globally; and secondly that these global effects could be understood by the application of geometric ideas

---

[8] Ibid, pp. 11-12.

(such as the conic sections of Euclidean geometry). The model of the universe that emerged was both rational and what we call *linear*, in the sense that small changes to the initial state of the system led to small changes in outcome, and that (as was later believed) knowing the exact state of every particle in the universe at an instant in time, we could predict the onward evolution of events with exact accuracy. However, as Newton himself said, he found a few more interesting pebbles on the beach, while the ocean of truth lay undiscovered before him.

If we consider a gas of particles in a container, we can begin to see why the Newtonian outlook begins to break down. James Clark Maxwell (of Maxwell's equations fame) did just this in the 19th century. By applying the Newtonian approach to a gas of "ideal" particles, he was able to predict the distribution of velocities of the gas particles. Building on this, Boltzmann (who committed suicide just before his ideas were endorsed and accepted by the general scientific community) introduced the idea of the entropy (or randomness) of such a collection of gas particles. He showed that entropy must inevitably increase, reaching its maximum value at the equilibrium state of the gas. If the gas is confined to part of the box, or part of the gas has a different temperature, then this state has lower entropy (because it has more order or structure). Thus at equilibrium, the requirement to have maximum entropy means that the gas must be spread evenly throughout the box and have a constant temperature.

OPEN SYSTEMS

Now, all of this analysis depends on the gas being isolated in its box from outside effects. This is what we call a *closed* system. What has been discovered since then is that many systems of interest are not closed, and are not in the equilibrium state. If a system is not closed, it is called an *open* system. This means that there is energy and/or information flowing into or out of the system. To take a very British example, imagine boiling some water to make a pot of tea. In order to see what is going on, we heat the water in a saucepan, rather than using the more traditional kettle. We put the pan of water on the heat (a gas ring). To start with, not much appears to happen (except perhaps some odd looks from other members of your family as you stare at the pan of water). The system, consisting of the pan and the water, is certainly an open system: we are deliberately putting energy in the form of heat into it; *energy is flowing across the boundary of this open system.* A *constraint* has been applied to the system, because heat is going in at the bottom, so the temperature at the bottom and top of the pan are different; that is the constraint we apply. In the early stages, turning up the gas slightly just increases this constraint slightly; the system is still in the *linear* state.

After a few minutes, however, something very interesting suddenly happens. We see on the surface of the water an ordered structure of cells. These are called *Benard cells* and they correspond to columns of water rising and falling in the saucepan. This represents large-scale and long-range order within our system, and is certainly not linear. The energy from the gas ring has been transformed into a type of order. Turn off the gas and the order dissipates. Only by constantly injecting energy into the system can the order be maintained. This new type of order is called a *dissipative structure.* It depends on the flow of energy across the system boundary in order to be sustained.

Before the Benard cells appeared, the water in the pan looked very boring—it was *homogeneous* or *symmetric*—and any part of

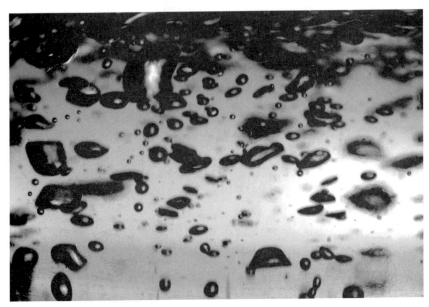

Rising columns of bubbles in boiling water

the water looked much the same as any other part. Once the Benard cells appear, however, we have structure—*the symmetry of the system has been broken.* These cells also rotate, and there is structure here too. If one cell rotates to the right, the next will rotate to the left. There is a *correlation* between what one part of the system is doing, and what another is doing. Even more intriguing is the fact that we cannot predict in advance whether a particular cell in a particular place will rotate right or left. *The system has multiple modes of behavior.* We are no longer in the linear world where one cause has one predictable effect. We have a *nonlinear system* where small changes in input can lead to large changes in effect. These behaviors, which we can see every day of our lives, pull the rug from under the Newtonian view of the world as a completely predictable system, if only we knew the initial conditions. As the number of possible modes of behavior multiplies, we head towards a *chaotic* system where the behavior can appear to be completely indeterminate and random, even though the underlying system is deterministic.[9]

Still under the sorry gaze of your family, you stare at the pan and continue to watch. Energy from the gas ring continues to pump into the system. Suddenly a new thing happens. The water begins to boil. The small elegant structures of Benard cells are swept aside and the whole pan of water bubbles. Chaos and turbulence have set in. We are no longer looking at local correlations across the system—this is a global effect across the whole volume of the water. It is caused by the local networks of bonds between hydrogen atoms being disrupted and then forming a global effect.

SELF-ORGANIZATION

Let us broaden our horizons from a pan of water to an entire ecosystem of interacting species of animals. In doing so, we increase the number of degrees of freedom of our system significantly. If the parts of our system still interact locally in a nonlinear way, then we transition from a chaotic system to a *complex* system with emergent behavior. If the local interactions are not of this form, then we have a system that is complicated, but not complex—the whole is the sum of the parts, and the behavior of the whole system can be understood by examining the parts. In a complex system, the whole is *more* than the sum of the parts, and thus we need to focus on the global emergent behavior of the system.

Sunlight flows into this complex system, and takes the place of our humble gas ring in the previous example, so our ecosystem

---

[9] Gleick, *Chaos: Making a New Science.*

is an open system. Of course, different species interact with each other, both within species and between species, in all sorts of complicated ways. They roam around, they fight, they compete for territories and mates—and they *coevolve*. Over the longer term, the environment also changes. In order to think this through, we need to boil all these interactions down to their simplest form.

Since Darwin, we have known that the key driver in evolution is the natural selection of the fittest. Thus, in its simplest form, we can ignore the other characteristics of an ecosystem of interacting species, and just focus on one thing. This is the way in which species evolve, and in so doing, affect the ability of "neighboring" species to survive. We call this *local coevolution*. *Neighboring* here means close in terms of species-to-species interaction and evolutionary effect. It does not necessarily (although it could) imply physical closeness.

The rest of this description follows that in Moffat,[10] while avoiding the mathematical details that just prove that it really does work like this. We can thus think of all of the species making up an ecosystem as being arrayed as the nodes of a grid, connected to each other by the lines of the grid, in order to capture this fundamental, local interaction between species. Figure 2.1 shows what this looks like.

If we plot the fitness of each species on this grid, we have a *fitness landscape*. How does this fitness landscape evolve over time? Each of the species can only interact with the species at neighboring nodes of the grid. Thus if the fitness of a species changes (for whatever reason), only the fitness of species at neighboring

---

[10] Moffat, *Complexity Theory and Network Centric Warfare.*

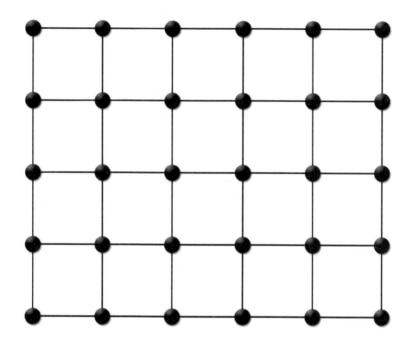

Figure 2.1: A schematic of the grid of interacting species in an ecosystem

nodes are affected. To start the system off, we just randomly assign a number (between 0 and 1) to each species that represents its relative ability to survive (i.e., its fitness in evolutionary terms). Now we let the ecosystem evolve through local coevolution.

Firstly we assume that the species with the smallest fitness is most likely to disappear and thus has the greatest pressure put on it to evolve. We thus scan across the fitness landscape (the grid) and find the species with the smallest fitness value.

Now we have to represent the evolution of this species and the resultant coevolving effect on the fitness of the neighboring

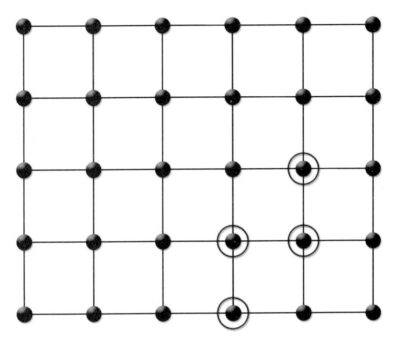

Figure 2.2: A network of size four of locally coevolving species within the ecosystem

species. Keeping things as simple as possible (but no simpler),[11] we do this by changing the fitness of the species and its next door neighbors on the grid by random values (so the new fitness could be higher or lower than it was before).

We scan across the grid again to see which species has the smallest fitness. If the same species or one of its neighbors is again chosen, then we call this a cluster or network of size one. Otherwise, we start with a new species at some other node on the grid.

---

[11] A concept articulated by Albert Einstein.

By repeating this process over and over again (on a computer) we can amass statistics regarding the size of such neighborhood networks. Each such network corresponds to a series of connections due to local coevolution of neighboring species (i.e., a ripple of coevolution across the grid).

The questions we want to consider are: What is the overall emergent behavior of such an ecosystem? Is it just some kind of meaningless chaos, or is there a higher order structure that emerges?

In fact, what happens is very surprising—a characteristic of the way in which higher level order can emerge from such a complex system. This is due to the large number of degrees of freedom of the system (i.e., the large number of species) and the local nonlinear interactions caused by coevolution. If there were only a small number of interacting species, the ecosystem would either produce rather predictable linear behavior, or else it would show evidence of chaos, with small changes to initial conditions leading to unpredictable and *disordered* behavior.[12] As we increase the number of species, we transition to a new type of behavior that we call *complex*. With a large number of species, we have a large number of degrees of freedom and as a result we get emergent *ordered* behavior. However, the ordered behavior that emerges for this open ecosystem, in which energy (sunlight) and information (the fitness of species) are flowing in and out of the system is entirely at odds with what we would expect from a closed system, such as a box full of gas particles.

As we discussed earlier, we know that a box full of "ideal" gas particles, starting in a random state without energy or informa-

---

[12] May, *Simple Mathematical Models.* pp. 459-467.

tion moving in or out of the box (so it is a closed system), will tend toward a state known as thermal equilibrium. This means that the final state of the system is homogeneous and symmetric. However, for our open ecosystem, in fact the *opposite* occurs. From an initially random state (remember we just allocated random fitness values to the species at each node of the grid), it *self-organizes* itself into a very ordered state. Here, all of the species in the ecosystem have a fitness value above a certain critical value (and we can calculate this value, it is strictly nonzero). This is equivalent to all of the gas in our box self-organizing to be only in part of the box, and dramatically illustrates the difference between closed and open systems. Our open system is far from equilibrium. A small nudge to the ecosystem will lead to a network of coevolution interactions that could be almost infinite in extent; whereas the closed system at equilibrium is resistant to change. A nudge to such a closed system (such as a fluctuation in temperature) leads to a rapid move back to equilibrium.

Systems that show these kinds of self-organizing, complex, and emergent effects are of particular scientific interest. They do not have any characteristic scale and can thus exhibit the full range of behavioral options within the system restraints. This means that such systems are in a position of optimal *flexibility* in some sense.

POWER LAWS

The next question that arises is: If the ecosystem can generate networks of interaction of all sizes, can we characterize in some way how often networks of a particular size arise?

Going back to our ecosystem, it turns out that the distribution of sizes of coevolving networks is a power law with a negative power value. This implies that there are likely to be a small number of large networks of coevolution, and lots of small ones created at or near to the self-organized critical point of the system. The answer is yes. To do this, we need to introduce the idea of a *power law*. This is a simple idea that is best described by a simple example. Suppose we have a number of piles of building blocks. We can define the size of the pile by the number of blocks in the pile. We then want to know how often we can have a pile of particular size. If this frequency is equal to the square of the number of blocks, then we have what is called a power law; in this case the power involved is two from the squaring relationship. Thus, a pile of four bricks will be present four squared times, which is sixteen times more often that a "pile" consisting of a single brick. In general, we can have any power value. If the power value is bigger than one, then larger piles are much more frequent than smaller ones. This starts to even out when the power value is between one and zero. If the power value is negative (i.e., less than zero), then smaller piles are much more frequently present than larger ones—this is in fact what normally happens. Small clusters or networks are normally much more frequent than large ones.

FRACTALS AND POWER LAWS

We say that an object has self-similarity if its characteristics are "similar" at different resolutions. An example is the Koch "snowflake." We start with an equilateral triangle. A third of the way down each side, we draw equilateral triangles sticking out, (with sides one third the original length). This figure now has twelve sides. Similarly, a third of the way along each of these sides, draw an equilateral triangle. By repeating this process as long as we please, we create a figure whose boundary is a fractal. This means that if we magnify or reduce it, its boundary still looks the same. We call this property *self-similarity*, and objects that enjoy this property are called *fractals*.

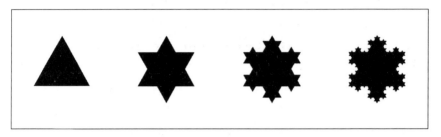

The Koch Snowflake

We have already seen, in our example of a complex ecosystem, the *correlation* in space or time between species as they locally coevolve. Correlation in space or time is a signal of local clustering and collaboration spatially, (e.g., within an open plan office environment) or in time (e.g., across an office intranet—reading email creates a correlation in time between individuals, taking a phone call creates a coincidence in time). The properties of fractals and their link to correlation have been examined intensively over the last two decades. To study them more closely, we now need to go on holiday. If you have small children, this means going to the beach.

THE SANDPILE MODEL

So there you are, lying on the sand in the sunshine, looking for something to exercise your mind. Testing yet again the patience of your family, you start to make a pile of sand (the sand is dry, that's why you are lying there). You make the pile by slowly dribbling sand through your fingers, rather like an egg timer.

At first, nothing very interesting happens. We are in the linear regime of system behavior where the system in this case is the pile of sand grains slowly growing beside you on the beach. The sandpile is an open system; energy in the form of additional sand grains is flowing into the system across the boundary. There are a large number of grains of sand, and they interact locally through nonlinear friction effects. In terms of our previous discussion, we know that the sandpile is potentially a complex system with emergent properties. The grains of sand interact locally with each other (one grain only interacts with the grains right next to it in the pile, like species in the ecosystem) and nothing surprising happens because, so far, these interactions are not rippling through the system.

However, something surprising does happen when the slope of the pile reaches a critical value. If we now add another grain of sand to our pile, the extra grain causes an avalanche (a cluster or network of local sand grain interactions), which is global—the effect reaches across the whole sandpile, or at least a significant portion of it. Local correlations between the grains of sand have turned into *global emergent behavior*, characterized by space and time characteristics such as the total number of sand grains involved in the avalanche and the time for which the avalanche lasts. These both form *power law relationships*. This means that if we plot the frequency with which an avalanche of sand of a particular size occurs, or for how long it lasts, then we get a power law plot. Normally the avalanches will be small, but occasionally they will be large. These large avalanches are ripples of local interaction cascading across the system.

There is more. If we plot the time and place at which each sand grain takes part in an avalanche, then our plot turns out to be a fractal. In a sense, we should expect this because our sandpile "system" has no preferred scale (large sandpiles act in the same way as smaller ones). Thus our plot should look the same at different scales (i.e., it should be a fractal).

WHERE HAVE WE GOTTEN TO SO FAR?

Let us pause on our journey through the ideas of Complexity to take stock and see where we have gotten to. We have now looked in some depth at the complex behavior of natural biological and physical systems. From our analysis of these open and dissipative systems, it is clear that there are a number of key properties of Complexity that are important. A list of these is given here.

1. **Nonlinear Interaction**. The interaction between neighboring entities is nonlinear. Small changes can have large effects.
2. **Decentralized control**. The natural systems we have considered, such as the coevolution of an ecosystem, are not controlled centrally. The emergent behavior is generated through local interactions.
3. **Self-Organization**. We have seen how such natural systems with a large number of degrees of freedom can produce extended ordered structure, without the need for guidance from outside the system.
4. **Non-Equilibrium Order**. The order (for example the space and time correlations) inherent in an open, dissipative system existing far from equilibrium.
5. **Coevolution**. We have seen how such systems are constantly coevolving. Clusters or avalanches of local

interaction are constantly being created across the system. These correspond to dispersed correlation effects in space and time, rather than a central imposition of large-scale coincidences in space and time.

6.   **Collectivist Dynamics**. The cascades of local interaction that ripple through the system.

SELF-ORGANIZING SOCIAL GROUPS

Self-organization in this context is taken to mean the coming together of a group of individuals to perform a particular task. They are not directed by anyone outside the group. This is not the same as "self-management," as no manager, outside the group, dictates that those individuals should belong to that group, what they should do, or how it should be done. It is the group members themselves who choose to come together, who decide what they will do, and how it will be done. A feature of these groups is that they are informal and often they are temporary. Enabling self-organization can often be a source of innovation. Some military commanders have always understood this: a commander must regard his superior's intention as sacrosanct and make its attainment the underlying purpose of everything he does. He is given a task and resources and any constraints, and within this framework he is left to make his plan. Critically, he is also expected to adapt to changing circumstances. Chapter 3 pursues this thought much further in the context of political and social systems.

Consider now the list of key concepts from Complexity Theory listed above, and see how they relate to ideas for the future—for *a new theory of warfare*. In this context, we first quote from Moffat in terms of thinking about the future:

In his recent book,[13] Dr. David Alberts, Office of the Secretary of Defense at the Pentagon, has placed the concept of 'network centric warfare' at the core of what the future of war might look like. The essential idea is that of a force structure which allows the 'edge' self-synchronization of autonomous units in the battlespace, in order to achieve specific mission objectives. These objectives are recognized through a shared awareness which all units have of the situation and of the overall goals to be achieved. What are the key drivers which have led him to this conclusion?

First, he is impressed by Alvin Toffler's argument that modern civilization has gone through three 'ages.' These, Toffler calls the agricultural age, the machine age, and the information age. The first of these was facilitated by the Neolithic agricultural revolution which domesticated animals and plants; the second by the Industrial Revolution, which harnessed steam and steel; and the third by the computer revolution, which has transformed the assemblage and processing of information.

Toffler also points out that in each age, warfare has been waged using the technology existing or emerging at that time: spears and arrows to guns; now from kinetic to non-kinetic forms of warfare; for as we move from the machine age into the information age, the same is true for us as it was for our forbears. Thus, Alberts asserts, the key technology for future warfare is the management of information.

---

[13] Alberts et al., *Network Centric Warfare*.

Self-organizing social groups

The second key driver was initiated by the fall of the Berlin wall. As we continue to peer through the dust of its collapse, the disintegration of the Soviet Union, and follow-on events, what we see is not one future, but a range of possible futures, characterized by uncertainty. This military uncertainty mirrors the economic uncertainty engendered by sharply interacting market-based economies.

From the commercial perspective, the reaction to such economic uncertainties has been to adopt institutional structures, which are much more flexible and adaptive to change. We have moved from the Dickensian hierarchy where Bob Crachett sat and shivered on his scribe's stool at the bottom of the heap, to the informed network (the flat management structure). Commerce too has been swept along by the forces identified by Toffler, and information is the glue which holds the future company together. We can see this happening in the use of company-wide Intranet services by organizations such as Shell and IBM, which span the globe.

Driven by the same underlying forces of increasing global uncertainty and transition to the information age, it is not surprising that the armed forces should consider more loosely based federations of functions to perform a mission in a self-synchronous way. This seems to be the essence of the network-centric approach. In this sense, the armed forces are not copying the commercial world: they are merely reacting in a similar way to similar forces of change. Flat command structures to maximize agility and force flexibility in response to the transition to the information age and uncertainty can be seen as inevitable from this perspective.[14]

We thus need to think in terms of the transition from the Industrial Age to the Information Age and the implications of that. In Table 2.1 is an interpretation in terms of an Information Age force structure of the key concepts of Complexity that we have considered.

Complexity Concept	Information Age Force
Nonlinear interaction	Combat forces composed of a large number of nonlinearly interacting parts.
Decentralized control	There is no centralized control dictating the actions of each and every combatant.
Self-organization	Local coevolution induces long-range order.
Non-equilibrium order	Military conflicts, by their nature, proceed far from equilibrium. Correlation of local effects is key.
Coevolution	Combat forces must continually coevolve in a changing environment.
Collectivist dynamics	Cascades of local effects ripple through the system.

Table 2.1: Relation between Complexity and a new theory of warfare

The nature of Network Centric Warfare for such future Information Age forces can be outlined as: within a broad intent and constraints available to all the forces, the local force units

---

[14] Moffat, *Command and Control in the Information Age*.

Self-organizing social groups

self-synchronize under mission command in order to achieve the overall intent.[15] This process is enabled by the ability of the forces involved to robustly network. We can describe such a system as *loosely coupled* to capture the local freedom available to the units to prosecute their mission within an awareness of the overall intent and constraints imposed by high level command. This also emphasizes the looser correlation and *non-synchronous* relationship between inputs to the system (e.g., sensor reports) and outputs from the system (e.g., orders). In this process, information is transformed into "shared awareness," which is available to all. This leads to units linking up with other units, which are either local in a physical sense or local through an information grid or intranet (self-synchronization). This in turn leads to emergent behavior and effects in the battlespace.

THE CONCEPTUAL FRAMEWORK OF COMPLEXITY

Prof. Murray Gell-Mann traces the meaning of *complexity* to the root of the word. *Plexus* means braided or entwined, from which is derived *complexus*, meaning braided together, and the English word "complex" is derived from the Latin. Complexity is therefore associated with the intricate intertwining or interconnectivity of elements within a system, and between a system and its environment. In a human system, connectivity means that a decision or action by any individual (group, organization, institution, or human system) will affect all other related individuals and systems. That effect will not have equal or uniform impact, and will vary with the state of each related individual and system, at the time. The state of an individual and system will include its history and its constitution, which in

---

[15] Alberts et al., *Network Centric Warfare*.

turn will include its organization and structure. Connectivity applies to the inter-relatedness of individuals within a system, as well as to the relatedness between human social systems, which includes systems of artifacts such as information systems and intellectual systems of ideas.

The term *complexity* is used to refer to the theories of Complexity as applied to Complex Adaptive Systems (CAS). These are dynamic systems able to coevolve and change within, or as part of, a changing environment. It is important however to note that there is no dichotomy between a system and its environment in the sense that a system always adapts to a changing environment. The notion to be explored is rather that of a system closely linked with all other related systems making up an "ecosystem." Within such a context, change needs to be seen in terms of coevolution with all other related systems, rather than as adaptation to a separate and distinct environment.

COMPLEX NETWORKS OF INTERACTION

There has been an explosion of research in the academic community over the last few years on the characteristics of networks.[16] Networks, in this context, cover everything from information networks to the Internet, the World Wide Web, the sharing of roles in Hollywood movies, and the interaction between cellular components in a metabolic system. We talk loosely about networking, meaning interacting with other people. That also is a form of network. How do we begin to make some kind of sense out of all of these types of networks?

---

[16] Albert and Barabasi, *Statistical Mechanics of Complex Networks.*

Let's start with some simple properties that all networks share. First, there is the idea of nodes. These are the Web sites on the World Wide Web (WWW), for example. They are the fundamental entities that interact with each other. Then there are the links. In the case of the Web, these are the hyperlinks between Web sites. If we choose a particular node of our network, there will be a certain number of links going out from that node, linking to other nodes of the network. We can count these links at the node, and we call this the *degree* of the node. If we do this across all nodes of the network, then we have a range of values of degree, which is called the *degree distribution*. For our example of the WWW, the degree of a Web site is just the number of other sites it is hyperlinked to. The interesting question for the WWW is: What is its degree distribution? We now know the answer to this—but more of that later.

In real life, there are many ways in which networks could arise. However, it turns out that there are three key different types of networks, and the degree distribution is one of the main ways we can tell one from another.

RANDOM NETWORKS

Now we are going to play a game. Imagine you have a blank sheet of paper. Spread across the paper are a number of dots. Choose two dots, and throw a pair of dice. If the dice add to 2, then join the dots, otherwise don't. Do this for every pair of dots. This is the simplest way of creating a network, and due to the use of the dice, we call it a *Random Network*. This was the first type of network to be analyzed sytematically, and indeed until a few years ago was the *only* type of network to be properly understood. The key question that was studied was:

As we make the *network size* (i.e., the number of dots), or the chance of making a link, bigger and bigger, do the properties of the network change, and if so, is this a smooth or a sudden change?

It turns out that in fact the key properties of the network (such as whether or not it is connected, i.e. whether you can get from any node to any other node by walking along the links) do change. What is interesting is that they change suddenly. What is even more interesting is that this sudden change can be related to something that happens in complex systems called *percolation*. To understand this, we need to put our piece of paper to one side, go outside, and consider a wall of rock.

PERCOLATION

If we look at a slab of crystalline rock, it is a mass of small grains. Some of these are porous (i.e., they allow water to seep through them) and some are not. As we gradually increase the proportion of porous grains, the chance increases that water will be able to flow—to *percolate*—from one side of the rock slab to the other. This is important in looking at oil or water flowing in rock beds, for example. It turns out that there is a certain critical proportion of grains such that below that, water cannot flow, and above it, water can flow all the way across. This is the percolation phase change effect. The sudden change in properties of a Random Network can be shown to be equivalent to this sudden type of phase change in percolation.

If we are given a network, can we tell if it is a Random Network?

Marble, a porous metamorphoric rock formed from limestone

Yes we can, and the key to it is to look at the degree distribution. But we also need to look at another aspect of the network called the *clustering coefficient*. This is a measure of how well-linked the neighbors of a given node are in the network.

In a Random Network, the average of the degrees of each of the nodes is easy to predict, based on standard statistical theory. If the number of nodes (i.e., the number of dots in our example) is large, and the chance of creating a link between two nodes (i.e., the chance of getting a sum of 2 on the dice in our example) is small, then this average degree is just these two values (number of nodes and chance of a link) multiplied together. So if there are ten thousand nodes, and the chance of a link is one in a thousand, then the average degree is about ten. There is a scatter about this value, because of the chance nature of making links using rolls of the dice. The shape of this curve is like a bell, rising smoothly to the average value, then going down smoothly beyond the average value.[17] This kind of shape is the signature of a Random Network.

SMALL WORLD NETWORKS

Until just a few years ago, we thought that Random Networks were the only kind of network that could be analyzed. However, recently there has been an explosive increase in interest in this area, and two further key types of networks have been discovered. The first of these is called a "Small World" Network. To understand what this means, we have to introduce another idea. Imagine that the U.K. is a network—a network whose nodes are all those currently living in the U.K. If two people know each other well enough to be at least acquaintances, then we define this as a link of the network. Research on such acquaintance networks indicates that if we choose two people at random living in the U.K., then the number of links across the network (i.e., the number of intermediate acquaintances that link one person to the other) is low—in some cases as low as six on average. This is at first sight very surprising, given the millions of people in the U.K., and the fact that we just chose two at random.

One reason that this occurs in a network is because there are a number of "shortcuts" across the network that link together clusters of communities that are otherwise isolated. As a network, what we have just considered is the average distance between two nodes of the network chosen at random. We call this the *average path length* through the network. Formally, if a network has a small average path length, and is highly clus-

---

[17] Formally, it is a Poisson Distribution.

tered (so it has a high "clustering coefficient"), it is called a Small World Network. This combination of small average path length and high clustering coefficient tends to produce networks that consist of essentially local communities that are highly interlinked, with a number of longer range links linking these local communities together. If the number of long range links is very small, the network is almost a collection of isolated communities (e.g., the villages of England prior to the use of proper roads). As the number of long range links increases, the network becomes more richly interconnected as a whole.

SCALE FREE NETWORKS

The third key category of networks focuses on how certain types of networks grow and evolve over time. When we considered Random Networks, the number of nodes (the number of dots to join) was given in advance. No longer. Suppose we have a few dots (say 10) on the paper to start with, linked in some way. Now a new dot is added (the network *grows)*. How does it link with the existing dots? We assume that a fixed number (say 2) of new links are added to the network, each starting from the new dot. Which dots of the existing network should we choose to link these to? Here comes the difference. The appeal of each of the existing dots is assumed to be proportional to the number of links it already has (i.e., to its degree). We choose our two dots on the basis of this *richness of connection*—the richer a node, the more likely it is that we will choose it. Because we are choosing nodes preferentially in terms of their richness of connections, this process is called *preferential attachment.*

If we continue adding more dots to the paper, each having two new links, and linking them into the existing network (all dots created up to now) using preferential attachment, what kind of network do we end up with? One way of approaching this is to look at the range of values of the degree of a node. For a Random Network, this gives a curve in the shape of a bell. However, for this new type of network we get something completely different—a *power law*. This means that the chance of a node having a certain number of links (its degree) is related to the number of links by a power value. We have already come across the idea of power laws in complex systems. It is no surprise that they also emerge from complex networks that have no preferred scale. This *power value* is a key characteristic of such a network. For this type of relationship, there is no bell-shaped curve with a well-defined highest point—there is thus no scale by which we can define the network. Because of this, such a network is called *scale free*.

NETWORK VULNERABILITY

Scale Free Networks tend to have a small number of richly connected nodes and a large number of sparsely connected nodes. This is because of the power law distribution of connectedness (degree) across the nodes of such a network. They are thus vulnerable to targeted attack of these "rich hubs," which can very quickly disconnect the network into fragments. However, if a node is attacked at random, it is unlikely to be one of these rich hubs (unless you are unlucky). Because of this, a Scale Free Network is more robust that a Random Network to such random attack. In a biological ecosystem for example, a random "attack" might be the equivalent of the random loss of species. Ecosystems are much more tolerant to such loss, but not to the loss of the most connected (keystone) species. When these are lost, the ecosystem decays quickly. Similarly, within a cell, the set of metabolic reactions is scale-free. This is then robust to "random attack" by DNA mutations.

The sea otter: a keystone species that controls the sea urchin population, thus protecting kelp beds and the ecosystem supported by them

Scale Free Networks appear to be widespread in natural systems, presumably because of this robustness to random errors or attacks. It has also been shown that both the World Wide Web and the Internet are examples of Scale Free Networks.

PATTERNS OF INTERACTION

Small World Networks, in general, have the same type of degree distribution (i.e., the plot of frequency of degree at a node of the network) as a Random Network. Thus, this cannot be used as a way of discriminating between them, although a network in transition from a Scale Free Network to a Small World (which we discuss in depth later) will have a longer "tail" in the degree distribution as the rich nodes (those with high degree) remain and then gradually disappear as the network changes over time.

What does discriminate between Small World and Random Networks is the combination of average path length (the average number of links in the shortest path between two nodes) and the clustering coefficient (which measures how richly connected the network is locally). In general, Random Networks have a low average path length and a low clustering coefficient, whereas Small World Networks have a low average path length but a high clustering coefficient.

COMPLEXITY AND CASCADING EFFECTS: A REAL EXAMPLE

In complex systems, as we have seen, one effect (such as the change in the fitness of a species) leads to a cascading of effects (such as the resultant coevolution of the fitness of other species in the ecosystem). Such cascading of effects results in either intended or unintended consequences. The cascading of *intended* effects can be considered to be an important part of what is now termed *Effects Based Operations*.

In simple terms, this expression means that in warfare, a blow is delivered to the enemy, which has an initial consequence, but it is the further cascaded intended consequences at both the *political and military levels* that are of importance, and are sought after. These effects, both physical and psychological, ripple through the system.

An example of this kind of coevolved effect is drawn from the experiences of author Jim Moffat when working as a young analyst in the Headquarters of the Ministry of Defence in London, in 1982. It is told in the first person for ease of description.

THE ATTACK ON PORT STANLEY AIRFIELD: THE FALKLANDS WAR, 1982

My office was on the first floor of the main headquarters building of the Ministry of Defence, in Whitehall, London, just opposite Downing Street. Back in 1982, I had just finished doing a piece of analysis to help decide the mix of weapons that should be procured for the Tornado ground attack aircraft, so I had established good links with the group of military officers in the building who had responsibility for such operations. Our bosses were away on business at the time (in the United States, as I recall) when an urgent message came down for me to have a meeting with the military. (This was just after the Argentine forces had invaded the Falkland Islands.)

The military officers had been asked by the Secretary of State for Defence to establish a way of attacking Port Stanley airfield using one or more Vulcan aircraft. This airfield was the one useful concrete runway on the Falkland Islands, and was being used by the Argentinean forces as one of their main links back to the mainland. The analysis had to be done in a matter of hours. They turned to me for advice.

A 1-star (high ranking) officer was immediately nominated as my point of contact with the military staff, and a senior MoD scientist peer reviewed my analysis before it was handed over to the 1-star. An Operations Cell to manage the initial response to the Argentinean invasion had been set up in the building on the fourth floor, and I was given direct access through two steel barred doors to the RAF Group Captain (an ex-Vulcan pilot) who was in control of this. His desk sat at the rear of a long, low room festooned with cables, TV monitors, and the desks of very busy people. In discussion with him, I established some of the parameters of the operation such as the height of the aircraft over the target. I then retrieved a large scale map of Port Stanley Airfield from the map store in the basement of the building, several floors underground. With some help, I rapidly established the name of the construction firm that had constructed the airfield in the first place and phoned them up. They gave me the precise composition of the runway surface (such as the thickness of the concrete and what was underneath it). Colleagues at the Royal Aircraft Establishment (as it then was) could then calculate for me the size of a crater made by a 1,000 lb. bomb dropped from a Vulcan.

The Group Captain worked out the potentiometer and intervalometer settings that would need to be used (this was not trivial because the Vulcan was designed to deliver nuclear weapons). This gave (with a bit of calculation) the spacing between the craters on the ground. The key question was then: Should we use 7, 14, or 21 bombs? The more bombs used, then the higher the chance of hitting the runway, of course. However, the more bombs used, the more weight and hence the more fuel required. Carrying 21 bombs meant a large number of refuellings of the Vulcan on its several thousand mile transit to the target. In fact, it meant refuelling aircraft refuelling other refuellers to get them into the right position to refuel the Vulcan.

I drew the bomb craters on three strips of plastic (seven on each strip) to the correct scale of the large map of the airfield, and wrote out my analysis of the chance of getting a bomb on the runway in terms of the number of bombs, the height of the aircraft and the angle of the aircraft track relative to the runway (all of which were important in deciding the final aircraft flight path). The senior scientist peer reviewed my calculations,

The attack on Port Stanley Airfield: The Falklands War, 1982

RAF Vulcan Bomber

and I then briefed the 1-star RAF air commodore. He told me later that this information was first briefed to the Secretary of State later the same day, and then briefed by the Air Commodore to the War Cabinet, chaired by Mrs. Thatcher, the Prime Minister (now Baroness Thatcher). Mrs. Thatcher herself played around with the strips of plastic and the map before declaring that 21 bombs would have to be used, and so it was decided. The attack went ahead, and one bomb struck the runway, as reported across the world's press and media the following day.

THE CASCADE OF EFFECTS

The immediate (military) effect was disruption of takeoffs from Port Stanley airfield. However, I was informed much later, by someone working in the embassy in Argentina, that in response to the attack, the Argentineans decided to withhold a significant proportion of their airforce back in Argentina in order to protect their home airfields. This was confirmed subsequently:

> Operation BLACK BUCK (as it became known) not only reached and bombed the targets but, in doing so, showed the Argentineans that the RAF had the potential to hit targets in Argentina. This forced them to move their Mirage fighters farther North, [thus preventing] Mirages from escorting the Sky Hawk attacks against the British, especially the RN and Merchant Ships in San Carlos Water. The Vulcan raids also impacted upon morale, damaging that of the Argentine forces but uplifting that of the British, especially before the landings at San Carlos. Furthermore, BLACK BUCK was considered a strategic success, forcing Argentina to re-deploy Mirage fighters to protect Buenos Aires.[18]

This then reduced the pressure of attacks on the Royal Naval task force *(cascaded military effect)*. At the political level, the consequent success of the task force (due of course to the brave men and women on board, many of whom gave their lives during that action) bolstered the Prime Minister's position in helping to confront the Soviet Union during the Cold War period *(cascaded political effect)*.

From this example, we can see then how a network of coevolving consequences occurred, and how they propagated not just at the military level, but at the political-military level.

---

[18] AP 3003, *A Brief History of the Royal Air Force.* pp. 271-273.

The cascade of effects

As is clear from the description, the way in which this work was carried out was through an informal task-based network. The formal hierarchy of the organization tolerated this way of working due to the scale of change with which it was dealing (the sudden shift from peace to war). This interaction between informal trust-based networks and the formal organization is one of the key aspects discussed in later chapters.

CHAPTER 3

POLICY THROUGH CHANGE[19]

Complexity ➡ Networks

In this chapter, we focus on some real and telling examples of how Informal Networks of interaction were created that complemented the formal institutional structures they were "blessed" by.

Writing in the London Times in 1939, George Orwell foresaw the left and right joining forces to fight the threat of Nazism as part of an ongoing revolution in British politics along socialist lines[20]—necessary "if the country were to pull together to win the war." From some perspectives, this joining of forces worked and Britain successfully resisted Nazism while avoiding internal "violent change." But that would be a superficial reading of both history and revolution. In many regards Britain did experience a period of "great change and reconstruction" at almost

---

[19] "Change is inevitable in a progressive country. Change is constant." Prime Minister Benjamin Disraeli, speech in Edinburgh, Oct 1868.

[20] As developed further in his essay: "The Lion and the Unicorn: Socialism and the English Genius." 1941.

every level of society and every sector as it fought first for national survival, and then engaged in the new international politics of the Cold War and post-colonialism. During these short 8 years, Britain moved from Empire to Commonwealth; from independence to co-dependence; international lead to subordinate; private to national; league to union—the individual to the collective.

Orwell had been proven right in many regards; it was the conscript armies of the Western and Soviet publics that produced the weapons, sailors, soldiers, and airmen necessary to wage total war. It was they who fought and won against the tyranny of Nazism, from Africa, Europe, and the Atlantic to the Pacific and the Far East. The young men and women who went off to fight as their fathers had before them returned to very different countries from those that had borne them. And they had changed too, as evidenced by the "Khaki Election" of 1945 when Churchill, the Conservative hero of wartime Britain, was rejected for Attlee, his Labour Deputy, and the social ideals of a Britain changed permanently. The new constructs might not have lasted long in the type of unfettered (interactive) international society of free people and trade envisaged by the Atlantic Charter of 1945, but the post-war peace rapidly solidified both states and societies[21] into the form of cohesive mass required institutionally to defeat and resist the threat now posed by the Soviet Union on an international scale.

It may be considered that changes to the ways in which we manage, organize, and govern ourselves tend to be evolutionary unless the threat posed is of such a scale as to necessitate

---

[21] As predicted by Churchill's address at Fulton, Missouri, heralding the fall of the "Iron Curtain" across Europe.

rapid change and make new connections. If we can understand how Britain dealt with the threat posed in 1939 and re-connected its resources over this period, albeit across and between the same institutional bodies, it may be possible to gain an understanding of how formal organizations and people may behave as they reorganize to face the new challenges of the 21st century.

INSTITUTES OF STATE

In the context of this work, formal organizations are considered essentially to be rule-based, linear, bureaucratic, and hierarchical constructs, whereas networks are taken to be trust-based, self-organized groupings—complex systems. Each can work across, within, and/or beyond the other, but both also need the other. Formal organizations and networks are not new. They have forms that have found expression from classical times onwards. This includes the period of the 12th and 13th centuries (as maintained by Paul Ormerod and Andrew Roach) during the Inquisition, between the organizations of the Holy Roman Empire and opposing "heretical"[22] networks (more of this particular example in chapter 4). Their relationship to power is also different. Whereas formal organizations act more as power capacitors, seeking to retain power within, they need networks to distribute that power effectively and efficiently. To be effective, networks work to create effects from their associated organizations.

So how do such organizations operate?

---

[22] Brooks, "Dangerous Liaison."

The departments of defense within a Western state can be broken down into four inter-linking levels,[23] which also have parallels across other government departments:

- The government with its senior policy makers and decisionmakers occupy the **grand strategic** levels of power with responsibility for resources including the economic and technical, and for setting out and delivering medium and longer term policies.
- Linking with government and advising upon grand strategic policies is the **strategic** level, populated by senior civil and military servants and advisers with responsibility for planning and applying resources in accordance with the grand strategic vision.
- The **operational** level is where, in military terms, Command is vested and is responsible for administering, implementing, and commanding campaigns and major operations to realize grand and strategic objectives.
- The **tactical** level is where the grand and strategic visions are effected—the sharp end, responsible for controlling and directing resources as commanded and in order to gain operational objectives.

If this hierarchy is working perfectly, the grand vision is broken down at the strategic level into the different policies necessary to deliver the required context and tools for the operational level to create the necessary effect at the tactical levels. Today, management gurus argue for "flat structures," and de-layered organizations where everyone knows their job, trusts each other, and can be trusted. It is this question of "trust" that in turn is linked to both scale and bureaucracy and so to the his-

---

[23] As outlined also by British Military Doctrine.

Institutes of state

torical—some say industrial—hierarchical management structures typical of the 19th century and the Industrial Age, as introduced in chapter 2. It is the question of trust that also besets government—for superimposed across the grand, strategic, operational, and tactical levels is the temporal—the policy cycle that, for most Western governments, repeats every 2 years.[24] This does not give much time for a government to implement policies and to verify/establish trust with the electorate between elections.[25]

Returning to the question of formal organizations and the purpose they fulfil, we need perhaps to ask ourselves what they do (or do not do) well. Formal organizations are not trust-based, which is not to say that they cannot be trusted or that we do not place our trust in them. But formal organizations can and do remain effective even when no longer trusted. For example, President Nixon's administration continued in office long after he had lost the moral and popular trust of the U.S. public. So, on the one hand, while formal organizations may be considered as non-trusts, on the other, a newly elected government, coming to power for the first time in many years,[26] needs to be able to trust in the organs of government without which it will be unable to govern. In democracies, this requires an apolitical civil (and indeed military) service capable of transcending party politics and bridging the differences between the incoming and

---

[24] In the U.S., U.K., Sweden, and Australia, there is a 2-year grand strategic decisionmaking cycle, and in between, new policies are planned, implemented, and affected.

[25] In the U.K., the government can call an election at any time within 5 years of coming to office. Other nations (e.g., the U.S.) have fixed terms of 4 years.

[26] For example, the return of the British Labour party to power in 1997 for the first time in almost 20 years.

outgoing parties. This, in turn, requires trust between the institutes of government and those elected.

In the U.K., the loyalty of the civil service is to Her Majesty The Queen as in the U.S. it is to The President, although in recent years it has been argued that this trust has been broken by the appointment of "special advisers" loyal to their political masters and not to the head of state. By implication, unlike formal organizations, political parties are fundamentally self-organizing and trust-based. When organs of government are not trusted by the incoming party, problems can arise—particularly in a democracy. The fact that the civil service is not elected means that while they are servants of the elected party, their loyalty is to the head of state. The organizations themselves were created by government to support government and to provide the tools for doing so over time and at a scale that could not be done by the party itself. They are not random. Because the organizations rely on the patronage of the government (in whom they must trust), they are institutionally and indeed constitutionally constrained from speaking out or disobeying the "lawful" government. The Nazi party is a case in point. Elected as a growing minority between 1928 and July 1932, it suborned both government and its organs to the will of the Führer (the de-facto head of state) and itself in a very short order, with little "organized" opposition.

It follows that formal organizations would appear to serve a purpose where a condition for their existence is the trust placed in them to fulfil a particular function over scale and time. For example, even in the most disparate, disaggregated, dispersed, and de-layered of organizations, the role of paying people in any business with five or more employees is usually highly formalized and often remote from the core business itself. Yet, with very little interaction we place our trust in these organizations to make our regular salary payments. Indeed, given the highly centralized payments made directly to the banks of British servicemen, the blow to a non-conscript service of a hacker attacking and stopping these payments could potentially be immense. A crucial trust would seem to have been broken or at least damaged severely.

Chapter 2 suggested that there are other ways by which we organize ourselves and to which we have given the broader term of *networks*. Networks are not new, but perhaps their ubiquity and strength has been revitalized in an information-rich and highly connected age, increasingly used to self-organize in order to get things done.

BACK TO THE FUTURE AND OUT OF THE WILDERNESS

Institutionally, the Allied armies that began the Second World War looked and fought very much like those that had ended the First, but there were differences too. Political inertia and entrenched resistance to the military (not so much pacifism as anti-militarism) since the end of the First World War had determined that any expenditure upon the armed forces was to be done cheaply; in effect reinforcing the "old and tested" over the "new and untried." The great military advances and lessons of the First World War in terms of command and control (air-land-sea), self-organization, air power from/to sea and land, submarine warfare, tanks, close support, and communications were largely ignored in favor of the static: the Maginot Line over Blitzkrieg and battleships over aircraft carriers.

But they were not overlooked by Germany and Japan. And in warfare, as in so much, it is not just about the equipment with which one fights, but more about the state of mind with which one fights. Not a return to the old French notions of élan[27] that saw so many French soldiers slaughtered unnecessarily in 1914 to outmoded tactics poorly supported and rigidly enforced, but a state of mind that is in itself agile and "maneuverist,"[28] expecting the unexpected and prepared to "adapt and overcome."

The British and certainly French forces in 1939 went to war expecting to sit in trenches alongside the French Army for the next 5 years while victory was "attritioned" out. The German Army did not.

When Churchill re-entered government in 1939, he was 65 years old and had spent much of the previous 10 years not just in opposition to government and his own party, but as an outcast from the establishment[29] and the perceived wisdom of the time. Here, after all, was the man who had resigned after the disastrous Gallipoli campaign, had "crossed the house" twice and had—through the introduction of the Gold Standard in 1926—caused great strain to British, Empire, and international trade. The welcome he was given by the Admiralty,

---

[27] Espoused originally by Foch in his prewar book *Les Principles de la Guerre* as a combination of "élan" and the "sureté" of the elements provided by firepower, discipline, and tactics to protect the "offensive á outrance," the idea was taken forward by Colonel Grandmaison and others as one of élan not of sureté—offence at the expense of defense.
See also: Tuchman, *The Guns of August*. pp. 32–36.

[28] British Army Doctrine.

[29] Not least from Queen Elizabeth, the Queen Mother, who regarded Churchill's earlier support for Edward VIII and pivotal advice during the abdication crisis with considerable misgiving.

heralded as it was by the famous signal "Winston is back" was not as well received as it may appear to imply[30] and his time as First Lord of the Admiralty was not particularly successful.[31] Yet, from 1940 onwards Churchill was able to influence the creation of almost every institute of worth[32] within Britain and beyond. Without the support of the Establishment that had largely resisted and even outmaneuvered him before the war, Churchill had to appeal to a wider polity—a polity, to their lasting credit, who had listened to Churchill and had come to trust in his wider international vision for the near future. It is this question of trust that is so fundamental and marks a significant difference between the organizations that frustrated him out of government and the trust placed in him by the greater polity when in government. Yet, it was these formal organizations who "blessed" Churchill, giving him the reins of power necessary to prosecute "total" war. And in 1945, it was the same polity that signalled a new trust by selecting a Labour government to lead the peace. Perhaps in 1940, the Establishment had little choice but to bless Churchill or seek compromise and possibly even base surrender by choosing Halifax at the price of breaking the trust of the people. By 1945, the Establishment had "anointed" Churchill as their leader, but by then new trusts had emerged by people anxious

---

[30] For a fuller account see: Jenkins, *Churchill*. Chapters 29–30.

[31] The Norwegian Campaign was, in Roy Jenkins' terms a "disaster." Certainly it could not be considered a success either at sea, through the losses of many ships including the aircraft carrier *HMS Courageous*, or on land, with retreat from *Narvik*. Interestingly, significant German naval losses were to lead to a much reduced role of the surface fleet than had previously been considered. Not perhaps as marked as the "post Crete" decision not to deploy German paratroopers from air again, but significant nonetheless.

[32] From those of the British Empire to the creation of the U.N. and NATO through to support for the European Steel and Coal Pact, that in turn led to the Common Market, the EEC, and thence to the EU.

to deliver peace and the same organizations had no choice but to reflect the will of the demos.[33]

RETURNING TO POWER

Churchill on his return to power may not have been trusted individually by many of his political colleagues and the civil and military services, but in a sense this was unnecessary; more important was his ability to work within government. In those early days, the Establishment served its purpose in allowing the transition of power from Chamberlain to Churchill and in the latter days, even when individuals were not won over, they supported his intent, effectively and efficiently. We talk nowadays about someone being a good "networker," of being "richly connected." Churchill was clearly that and he continued to develop new connections throughout his life. Although he brought into office some specialists in the spring of 1940,[34] he quickly reached out to establish a remarkable coalition government consisting of standing Labour and Tory MPs, military and civil servants, indeed placing much of his trust in the opposition Labour Party. Until late 1942, it was opposition from his own back benches that was of most concern[35] to him. Churchill was able to encourage a series of highly connected clusters, each branching out from him and cascading across the levels of government.

---

[33] The will of the people; the personification of democracy.

[34] e.g. Brendan Brackan, Lord Beaverbrook, and Baron Solly Zuckerman.

[35] Churchill won a vote of confidence debate in early 1942 after the fall of Singapore but on the back of bringing the U.S. successfully into the war on Britain's side following the Pearl Harbor attack in December 1941. However, the censure debate he faced in July 1942, following the fall of Tobruk, was much more serious and led from the Tory benches.

Arguably, Churchill had a remit for change and the urgency of the moment gave him access that few peacetime Prime Ministers would be afforded, or indeed, need or demand. This, perhaps, is another temporal perspective of formal organizations. Not only do they operate over time, where managing the continuum is an important factor, but, because they are scaled, they also can cause (if not effect) change quickly when the imperative to do so is sufficiently high. Therein lies another distinction between formal organizations and networks, for while it was the Establishment that blessed Churchill, it did not effect change directly but encouraged clustered Small World Networks[36] to form, so to do. Hierarchies need a rule set to run by and by applying this set of widely understood and trusted rules, they become excellent bodies for preserving scaled constitutional arrangements and managing the status quo. (We use "scaled" here to indicate control over the number of connections between one member and another in the organization.)

This very rule set—itself constructed to suit a particular moment and context—is not intended to be easily adaptable. In a legal setting, these rules are usually open to wider interpretation, acting effectively as buffers beyond which interpretation is no longer permitted (within the meaning of the law). And to interpret the law, we usually create a Small World Network of jurists and the judiciary to bound its flexibility, limits, and meaning. On the one hand, we have the institutes of law and law making, with all their associated powers, and on the other a networked arrangement for interpreting and applying (not enforcing) the law. Beyond the judiciary, there are organs of law enforcement responsible for directly implementing the decision

---

[36] By a Small World Network, we mean a network of highly interconnected individuals (high clustering coefficient) who can easily interact with each other (small average path length through the network). See chapter 2.

of the courts, without interpretation, and in accordance with the wider previously ordained rights and rules of the individual. This move from network to formal organization to network and so on may in fact be the norm. In government, the Small World (party) Network that assumes power then uses formal organizations to deliver and exercise power. However, formal organizations when confronted with significant change often create more loosely coupled networks. These networks, blessed by formal organizations, exist for a specific reason or function for managing complex change. Although networks may be quickly created, they can take many years to fade away, provided that the mutual trust upon which they are based has not been broken and key players remain connected. Networks serve specific functions. Once these are completed, or their remit exhausted, if they are to preserve purpose over time and require to do so, they need to transfer their rules to a suitable custodian—normally back to a formal organization.

Formal organizations and networks can be permanent structures but their costs vary greatly. An institute or body of laws can exist to give expression to rules even when there is no call upon them. The Football (soccer) Association (FA) and its member clubs continue to exist and to function over the summer months even when the season has ended. Yet the teams no longer exist practically—the momentary networks in which players have been brought together to play no longer exist tangibly—as the club continues to. When the players return at the start of the next season they form into new teams, with new players. The scaled FA and the clubs, as formal organizations, pervade over time whereas, by contrast, their teams fade away continually, like old soldiers. Certainly, except when a member ceases to exist, teams continue to "be" although in a vital and formal sense they cease to "be" once the club "dispenses with

Some organizations may only come together on certain occasions

their services." By contrast, a club declared bankrupt ceases to "be" in any tangible or reconfigurable way, its assets permanently dispersed and lost to memory.

Formal organizations exist to embody and empower a scaled rule set and exist, de jure. Networks do not need a rule set to exist: they can and do exist, de facto. But, networks need recognition from formal organizations if they are to have resources and effect. The football team at the start of the season is brought together by the legal entity of the club and is blessed by it—the team now has the legal authority to represent the club. Yet networks can exist without formal organizations. The Sunday afternoon soccer team comes together spontaneously: not because members have been ordered to, but because the context in which they play is known, a priori. But, if they are to progress through a "Sunday League," they need a rule set to do so. By contrast, formal organizations cannot rely on self-organizing, spontaneous gatherings—they need a context in which to gather and the rules and power to control, not the game, but the occasion and moment of it. The team (or network) plays the game; the club (or organization) plays the rules.

The de facto and de jure relationships between playing the game and playing the rules and the context in which formal organizations and networks exist are essential to their understanding. In Bosnia, Kosovo, Sierra Leone, Afghanistan, and Iraq a pre-condition of peace and reconstruction has been the re-establishment of law and order necessary to give a society back the trust needed to start rebuilding—when the roofs start going back on and people start making bricks[37] and mortar again. Within government, a similar set of contexts and trusts need to exist. At the grand strategic level resides a Small World Network of politicians and senior advisers whose power is exercised by the institutes of state, existing at the strategic level. The strategic levels also bless the operational levels, enabling them to carry out their bidding and they in turn bless the tactical level. This is a type of top-down, institutional approach more reminiscent of the Industrial Age. In practice, networks and formal organizations exist in different shapes, sizes, and groupings across, between, and at every level—one scaled, the other more likely to be scale-free. Returning to the idea of networks playing the game and formal organizations playing the rules, it is also a question of from where one is looking. To a network at one level blessed by a higher organization, the organization is the rule giver and provider—the network plays its game within the rules provided. Yet, within the organization itself other Small World Networks exist, blessed by the organization to have influence, not necessarily power, over its rule (or policy) making. Rules within games and games within rules. It is these relationships between formal organizations and networks, intra and inter alia, that are key to managing change successfully. Formal organizations that cannot change to ensure that their

---

[37] "Finally you can believe in the brick maker, alone with his five year old son in downtown Kabul: 'We have a government now. People need houses.'" Ignatieff, *Empire Lite*. p. 108.

context remains trusted will not endure—to endure they need networks to influence and lead change. Networks without power do exist and endure (they may fade away), but to be effective, they need the blessing of formal organizations.

INTO OFFICE AND ALL AT SEA

Churchill knew before 1939 how badly prepared Britain was. If the Battle of Britain was a close run thing, the battle for survival before America and the Soviet Union entered the war against Germany was to be a closer run thing yet—indeed it was to regularly keep Churchill awake at night. But for Churchill to be effective, he required the Establishment to trust him, allowing for others to play the game to a new set of rules—rules that they would need in order for the U.K. to survive in some future context, moment, or time. Churchill did not always play by the rules—he made mistakes, failed, and disenfranchised significant elements of his cabinet—but he played the game. This is also perhaps an important element of the relationship between formal organizations and networks. Whereas formal organizations often cease if they fail, networks can exist and fail, even exist *to* fail. Networks are expendable in a way that an institute may not be, giving the possibility for disposability, collapsibility, and the re-shaping of constructs from within. Failure is also inimitably associated with risk and proportionality, particularly with regard to decisionmaking and policy making. In his examination of Party-Army relations in Mao's China, Fang Zhu concludes that:

> ...the more authoritarian the regime, the more focused the elite will be on power and status rather than policy making. Candid policy debates require strict legal and procedural protection, without which it

is simply too risky for elites to act solely on their ideological convictions and policy concerns.[38]

In other words, Zhu observed that "without the legal and procedural protection" of the People's Republic of China, a context in which "the elite" could meet to "debate" their "ideological convictions and policy concerns" would not exist. It was the formal organizations of Mao and the PRC that needed to bless such a Small World Network of the elite with the safe context necessary for "candid policy debate." Thus, in blessing a network, formal organizations also need to provide the authority and power for creating *and* protecting its networks, whilst accepting the risk of failure to itself. In some instances, crucially those involving high personal risks, a network will not form unless protected by its associated organizations. This also brings another tension, for if a formal organization can fail, it needs to be able to recognize its risks of failure. So, although a formal organization may embed within it post-modern rules that deny any single truth, the one truth it must always be aware of and protect (through gatekeepers and gamekeepers) is that of its own existence. Whilst we might deny individual culpability or responsibility, formal organizations need always to remain acutely aware of their own truth and accountability for failure: where the buck stops.[39]

By extension, networks become a necessary part of successful organizations—directly, or in association, allowing them to test, interpret, and develop the rules and truths embedded within them. Mao's China did not allow for its ideologies and convictions to be exposed to "candid policy debate." As a

---

[38] Zhu, *Gun Barrel Politics*. p. 229.

[39] Unattributed Memo on President Truman's Desk.

Into office and all at sea

result, the Party was not strengthened or annealed through policy debate. Instead it was stultified and made brittle through competing factions within the party, the army, and the political elites.

The Battle of the Atlantic[40] was a struggle for Britain's survival and so the successful prosecution of the war. Churchill knew in 1940 that Britain could not defeat Nazi Germany alone, but in 1940 it was only Britain and its Empire that stood against Hitler. To remain in the game until the mantle could be transferred to the U.S. and the Soviet Union, Britain had first to survive. To do this, it needed to preserve the flow of munitions, personnel, and materiel to and from Britain, the Empire, the battlefields of Africa and the Mediterranean and, above all, the United States and Canada. Managing flow is relatively easy, being rule-based over time it is simpler to codify. What it is not so easy to create rules for is the management of connections or "choke points" or hubs, be they ashore or at sea. Choke points would provide the asymmetric vulnerabilities that Germany needed to attack if it were to defeat Britain.

Over recent years a myth[41] has grown that victory in the Atlantic was the result of Ultra and the work of Bletchley Park. In his book Decoding History, W.J.R. Gardner addresses the myth and concludes that:

---

[40] A phrase, like that of the Battle of Britain, devised by Churchill to describe a series of complex military and civil campaigns and skirmishes, spread over time and space. One of Churchill's many strengths was to give common expression and identity to otherwise complex concepts.

[41] Winterbotham, *The Ultra Secret*. This first broke the Ultra story—a story subsequently developed in literature and film.

... it is difficult to sustain the argument that Ultra was a critical factor at a sufficient number of levels and times to say that it was a factor of great, far less ubiquitous, criticality. This in no way denies either [its] utility or purpose...whilst Ultra was no mere member of a chorus but neither was it a star shining above all others—[there] were other spear carriers and... actors.[42]

The Battle of the Atlantic was a complex series of many different civil and military campaigns that cut across and connected every level of government, society, and the economy requiring the close coordination, command, and control of resources, manpower, and materiel at the grand, strategic, operational, and tactical levels. So how did the organizations of 1940 cope with this challenge?

One response might have been to create a command type economy with the center orchestrating and controlling the different spears and actors down to the nth degree. This was the response adopted by both Stalin and Hitler with control from the center strengthening over time in order to meet particular shocks and challenges. It has great advantage when the problems are not complex and the solutions relatively straightforward, linearly probabilistic, and easily understood.[43] But, over time it weakens the "edge" or peripheral organizations as power is subsumed to the center and the control

---

[42] Gardner, *Decoding History*. p. 218.

[43] The Soviet Great Leap Forward and post-WWII rearmament and even the space program and the German rebuilding and rearmament in the 1930s were greatly needed to repair the damages caused by war and revolution. Putting people back to work and injecting capital these programs created more work and injected growth through Keynesian principles.

necessary to define every perturbation within an economy becomes excessively bureaucratized, slowing everything down, removing individual initiative and substituting control of quantity for quality[44] and mass.

Britain instead set about encouraging a series of networks, including within them "heretical hubs"' such as Bletchley Park. Their task was to start working on the problem of how to identify, interpret, manage, and overcome the choke points at sea and ashore. For example, from 1940 through almost to the end of the war, the great London docks became untenable and it was necessary to route convoys through Liverpool. This in turn required the transport system to be re-routed from London to Liverpool, Belfast, and the Clyde. Given also the vulnerability of London and the southeast, it also meant dispersing essential manufacturing industries and dockers from predominantly the south and the Midlands to locations harder to target, preferably west of the Pennine Mountains in places like Manchester, Glasgow, and Belfast,[45] whilst ensuring that materiel and products were delivered. The complex nature of this whole-scale reorganisation could not be achieved without the initiative and self-organizing support of all sectors of society—it could be ordained, influenced, and blessed, but not controlled.

Churchill "was constantly initiating, asking why programs were not fulfilled, why there were so many people on headquarter

---

[44] So broken had the Soviet system become that by the 1980s in one famous case, 1,000 tons of nails was misinterpreted as a 1,000 ton nail, which was considered to be acceptable on delivery!

[45] Both Plessey and Ferranti developed large factories in and around Manchester during and after the Second World War, whilst Shorts of Belfast developed a niche in missile manufacturing and light aircraft design.

staffs…"[46] People were inspired by Churchill. He was able not just to empower the various networks with a sense of mutual trust but to give them both a sense of urgency—*action this day*—and a shared greater vision. He could also destroy trusts ruthlessly and sometimes mistakenly.

Alanbrooke makes some interesting comments in his diaries. He found Churchill infuriating to work with because of his hare-brained ideas and love of bypassing authority. However, he also admitted that Churchill's energy and charisma were vital to the war effort by stimulating the public and the formal organizations. In 1942, Alanbrooke was offered the chance to take over as CinC Middle East (which Alexander took instead), but refused because he thought himself the only man who could corral Churchill. Nevertheless, Churchill's overriding "Command Intent" provided a trusted context within which many networks could exist—and initiatives thrive. Eventually this system of "small world committee networks" was to extend beyond Britain and the Empire to include the Allies—even at its peak attempting, through Churchill himself, to accommodate the Soviet Union. Perhaps, by then, the basic trusts upon which the committee structures were founded had been over-extended and their efficacy began to dwindle. But at its most effective, this system was able to develop the capabilities and capacities to link both sides of the Atlantic into an effective war winning machine, capable of winning the Battle of the Atlantic and taking the war to the enemy. It probably also formed the basis upon which the Atlantic Charter, the UN, and NATO were founded.

---

[46] Jenkins, *Churchill.* p. 644.

Into office and all at sea

The Battle of the Atlantic was not won decisively—with the enemy wiped from the sea. It was won incrementally—with Allied and enemy forces continuing to face each other across the Atlantic right through to the defeat of Germany in 1945. In this type of close run series of indecisive skirmishes, flowing across land and sea, victory was more about one side losing than the other winning. Ultimately, an attritional battle of wills and capabilities developed, where victory would depend upon an accurate aggregated (stochastic) assessment[47] and understanding of successes and, as important, defeats.

The position in Germany was almost a complete reversal of that pertaining in Britain. Hitler's Germany did not have a tradition of government through committee and compromise, typical of most mature democracies,[48] where power is based upon knowledge and upon the sharing of information and knowledge between bodies—a type of percolation (see chapter 2) with vacuums and overpressures causing knowledge and information to flow between the different linked committee networks: each one trusting in the other and in its own authority to act. In the Third Reich, the allocation of resources and policy responsibilities was based upon *Führerprinzip*—controlled (*Befehlstaktik*[49]) through and by the Fuhrer. This created a situation where information was power[50]—*focusing the elite on power and status, (not) policy making*

---

[47] Operational Assessment within Britain's MoD grew out from the demand for accurate pol-mil-civil assessments required to inform strategic decisionmaking from the Battles of Britain and the Atlantic onwards.

[48] For example, the process of "pork-barrelling" to settle economic differences between U.S. states and accounting for transfers of billions of dollars is based upon close networks of trust, based upon a common trust.

[49] *Befehlstaktik* being detailed order, tactics, and control, as opposed to *Auftragstaktik*.

[50] "Power is not a means, it is an end—one makes the revolution in order to establish the dictatorship." Orwell, *Nineteen Eighty-Four*. pt. 3, ch 3.

Rather than being based upon trust, the Third Reich consisted of competing and overlapping organizations, each jealously guarding its own constitutional rule-base. The candid policy debates necessary to make sense of a complex, hostile environment and, crucially, to learn from failures, not just successes, simply could not exist. Without this type of environment, it was simply "too risky for [the] elites to act solely on their ideological convictions and policy concerns."[51]

In a tactical environment, where decisions were relatively straightforward, *Führerprinzip* provided the type of rapid and directed decisionmaking upon which *Blitzkrieg* was based, proving decisive in 1940 and in 1941. In the complex strategic environment of the Atlantic and that which unfolded in Russia, the system began to unravel. Information became ever more filtered, ever more dangerous to the messenger. Hitler refused to acknowledge the consequences of his own actions, and the German people realized far too late that they were trapped by a terrifying confusion (and complexity) of cause and effect.[52]

EFFECTS BASED OPERATIONS AND THE BATTLE OF THE ATLANTIC

To win the Battle of the Atlantic, the Germans needed to target accurately Allied choke points. This meant:

1. a coordinated bombing and (maritime) mining campaign that disrupted the flow of materiel to and from northwest England to the rest of the country and the Empire;

---

[51] Zhu, *Gun Barrel Politics*. p. 229.

[52] Beevor, *Berlin*. p. xxxiv.

2. a coordinated intelligence gathering campaign that accurately identified congestion/choke points (or hubs and clusters);

3. a political campaign to stop, or at least minimize, support from the U.S. to the U.K.;

4. a combined campaign to deny Allied air cover over crucial choke points;

5. a targeted maritime campaign, in enemy and international waters—balanced carefully against maintaining U.S. neutrality; and above all,

6. accurate political, diplomatic, and economic "effect" assessments (as opposed to battle damage assessments alone) that enabled the overall targeting of resources, maintaining the aim and the flow of men and materiel in a coherent and coordinated way.

To do this would require not only linking across the grand, strategic, operational, and tactical levels of government, but also between those levels—not just reducing their decision-making cycle times, but also making more good decisions than the enemy.

It is sometimes assumed that the Germans had a less capable intelligence gathering, surveillance, and analysis system than the U.K. The truth is somewhere between: in almost every sphere, from *sigint*[53] through to electronics, decryption (if not encryption), communications, aircraft, ships, submarines, armour, military production, and the quality of fighting manpower and operational/tactical leadership (*Truppenführung*: troop leadership or unit command), the Germans were supe-

---

[53] Signals Intelligence—which includes direction finding (DF) and spectrum analysis as opposed to decryption.

rior to Britain—*über alles*. Churchill knew this.[54] He also knew that the only hope for Britain lay in bringing in the United States on Britain's side. The only advantage that Churchill had, although probably he did not know it at the time, was Britain's capacity to create the self-organizing committee structures and Small World Networks necessary to orchestrate a complex four-level[55] battle in the timelines necessary; for the time needed before the Americans could join the fray. It was going to be damned close.

The Battle of the Atlantic was an attritional battle of capability and will upon which the analysis of tonnage sunk would prove crucial. To achieve an accurate assessment of the U-boat campaign, GrossAdmiral Doenitz needed an objective flow of operational data from his U-boats deployed tactically in the North Atlantic. Such objectivity is based essentially upon trust and the veracity of trusted individuals to make robust estimates. In the heat of battle, this can be particularly difficult to achieve—as seen by claims made, awarded, and later revised downwards during and after the Battle of Britain. However, if formal organizations need this type of veracity, then they need to encourage it. Preferment of German U-Boat captains and crews was based almost entirely upon a tonnage tariff that created a systematic, possibly systemic bias, probably in the order of at least ten to twenty percent[56] more than was actually sunk.

---

[54] Indeed in 1942, he openly questioned the fighting spirit of the British soldier, which, after the fall of Singapore in 1942, he considered much less than their fathers [in the 1914-18 war].

[55] Across the grand, strategic, operational, and tactical levels and the diplomatic, information, military, economic, and political environments.

[56] Gardner, *Decoding History.* p. 49.

USNR aircraft attacking and sinking U848, 1943

On entering the war, Britain had an estimated 20 million tons[57] of shipping and an additional 4 million tons under charter. German estimates for the sinking of British shipping, made as late as 1941, indicated a requirement to sink 800,000 tons a month[58] to take Britain out of the war, if not to submission. In broad terms, this would have meant reducing British and Allied ship-building and British flagged and chartered shipping capacity by between eighty and ninety percent in the crucial 2 years between mid-1940 and mid-1942. In fact, this monthly figure for tonnage sunk was only neared once, in June 1942.[59]

[57] Gardner, ibid. Amalgamating data from Adams in Howarth and Law, 160, Table 3 and Behrens, Appendix VIII.

[58] Gardner, ibid. p. 49.

[59] Gardner, *Decoding History*. p. 49.
    Fuehrer Conferences on Naval Affairs. pp. 334-335.

Crucially, to achieve such a strategic victory over Britain, Germany required, at all costs, to keep the U.S. and its potential ship-building capacity[60] out of the war until at least mid-1942.

By Doenitz's own reckoning,[61] toward the end of 1942, a submarine was sinking only 200 tons per day at sea compared to 1,000 tons a day in 1940. In 1940, to have achieved his target, Doenitz would have needed about 75 submarines to preserve 25 in the Atlantic at any one time—by mid-1942, to sustain a submarine loss rate of only ten percent and to make up for over-reporting, he would have required sustaining 400 boats to keep 130 on station. Consequently, Germany would have required building, equipping, and crewing on average 20 submarines a month from mid-1940 to mid-1942. From about 80 boats at the beginning of 1941 Germany had over 250 submarines by the end of the year[62]—a threefold increase but a vital twenty percent short of the numbers needed to defeat Britain by mid-1942. By early 1943, Germany had a submarine fleet of some 400,[63] but the hinge year of 1942 had been turned—production was falling and Britain was still in the fight, joined now by the U.S.

Tactically and operationally, Doenitz had the upper hand through to the end of 1942 and into spring 1943.[64] But, from the beginning, Britain held the grand and strategic advantage,

---

[60] Rising to over 8 million tons a year in 1942, from less than 1 million in 1941.

[61] Gardner, ibid. p. 63.
   Fuehrer Conferences on Naval Affairs.

[62] Gardner, *Decoding History*. p.19.

[63] Van der Vat, *Standard of Power*. p xviii.

[64] Towards the end of 1942 the monthly tonnage sunk had reached 500,000 tons a month, falling to 300,000 tons a month in May 1943, thereafter to 150,000 tons and thence to 100,000 tons a month in 1944.

which it never surrendered. Today we would consider a "network of networks" placing a "net" across the Atlantic, consisting of sigint, decryption, radar, aircraft patrols, shipping, escorts, docking and undocking facilities, strategic foreign policy, dispersed industries, and trade all feeding stochastically[65] to the analysts and all connected and sensitive to "Churchill's Intent." Not one factor was the more important—each network had to be trusted to know what was required of it, and to be rewarded accordingly. Not preferment based upon tactical success but upon the knowledge, veracity, and trust of being part of an esteemed close knit team, all reliant upon each other with the confidence to express their truth and be listened to. Churchill achieved this *personal touch*. The contrast with Nazi Germany could not have been more profound. The institutional rule bases created around the Fuhrer were never trusted by Hitler and there was little trust between him and his formal organizations. They were automatons—good at doing the bidding of Hitler and excellent at managing the "flow" of linear tactical and operational decisions (*Truppenführung*), but hopeless at addressing or understanding the type of connected, complex, nonlinear choke point *effects* they needed to.

Worse still, Nazi organizations were based upon fear and the fear of failing. Unlike Churchill, Hitler never was told enough to allow him to worry about grand and strategic policies for the Atlantic, let alone keep him awake at night. Perhaps, if he had been, history would have been very different, for to have won the Battle of the Atlantic, and very probably the war, Germany had at all costs to keep America neutral at least until the middle of 1942. Hitler, by declaring war on America after the

---

[65] Governed by the laws of probability and complexity and not by simple linear probabilities alone.

Japanese attack on Pearl Harbour, took away that moment for achieving a tactical victory/effect in the Atlantic—with all its grand and strategic implications. Six months later and it may have been a very different story.

BREAK OUT

The story of the Battle of the Atlantic did not finish until the end of the war, but from May 1943 onwards, when Doenitz ordered his submarines out of the Atlantic following the loss of his son and five submarines in a single action with nothing to show, it moved into its final phases. This time Churchill's aim was to open up the long demanded Second Front in the west. Timing would be crucial and Churchill was determined not to go until he and the Allies were ready. Despite huge pressure from Roosevelt and Stalin and perhaps strengthened by the setback of the disastrous Dieppe Raid in 1942, Churchill was able to hold off until he—and the Allies—were ready.

This was risk-taking at its highest level. Churchill first entrusted a junior Royal Engineer Officer to come up with workable plans and then blessed the designs and approved the manufacture of two entire docks to support the American and the British/Canadian landings. First, Churchill took the risk of bypassing his immediate colleagues and senior officers (not for the first time) to locate a (suitably connected junior military) engineer to work on the project and then, on his advice, he took the huge grand and strategic risk of transferring Britain's ship-building industry to dock construction, in what was to become the largest single civil-engineering endeavour in Britain's history.

At the same time as he convinced his cabinet colleagues to make this decision, he also had to persuade Roosevelt both to delay the invasion until 1944 and to take up Britain's further reduced capacity for ship-building—with its entire grand and strategic implications. All this at a time when the Battle of the Atlantic had yet to be won, against the prevailing wisdom of many senior British and American officers, President Roosevelt's 1944 election campaign, the Pacific versus European debate, and all in very short order. In April 1943, at Churchill's insistence, work began in secret on developing what were to become known as the "Mulberry Docks." The reasons for Churchill's personal involvement went back to failure at Gallipoli, reinforced by recent experience of the Dieppe Raid and his determination that success on the beaches of Normandy required a decisive tactical victory supported immediately by a strategic build-up and onslaught through France to Germany. To achieve this, he required the adaptability and agility to move vast strategic stockpiles of men and materiel from the U.K. to France and beyond. Tactically, this convinced Churchill of the need to have an expeditionary shipping point of disembarkation to have the *effect* of moving troops and equipment across the beachhead, autonomously, without the need first to capture ports and infrastructure.

An interesting example of the Soviet network of sympathetic Britons from across the social spectrum (and which persisted in one form or another well into the 1970s), then operating at Stalin's direction, was the outspoken demand for a Second Front to relieve the pressure on Russia—Stalin was fearful that the U.S. and the U.K. would let Russia bleed white before they came in to win the war and reparation. I (SRA) can remember, as late as the early 1970s, seeing an example of their graffiti on the railway arches between Putney and Queenstown Road stations in South London, demanding the "2nd Front Now."

Thirteen months later, Churchill had his two Mulberry Harbors operational on the Normandy coast and, in those vital few days whilst the Germans awaited the expected onslaught in the Calais area,[66] with "Pluto" (the sub-channel fuel pipe-line) they provided the strategic build-up of tactical *effect* necessary to prevent the Germans from driving the allies back into the sea. By the time of the great storm of the 19th of June, which destroyed the American Mulberry Harbor, the allies were beginning the break out and on the 30th of June, the Americans captured the much damaged port of Cherbourg. Designed to last only 6 weeks, the British Mulberry continued to support the allies through to November 1944, when Cherbourg came "on line."[67]

EXPERIMENTATION

In modern terms, we might consider the production of the Mulberry Docks as a worked example of Experimentation—by which, in a policy sense, one would mean the testing of different concepts and ideas so as to inform grand and strategic decisionmaking in order to deliver timely tactical and operational effect. Experimentation, as regarded currently in the U.S. DoD and the U.K. MoD, is necessary to make better, more agile policy decisions, reduce grand to tactical risks, and so as to *enable capabilities* and create desired *effects* in much

---

[66] Reinforced through the deception operation "Bodyguard," which included the fake "First United States Army Group (FUSAG)" under Lieutenant General Patton, until he took command of the U.S. 3rd Army in Normandy.

[67] "Eventually, Cherbourg would take more than half of all the cargo landed in France for American forces." Weinberg, *A World at Arms*. p. 689.

reduced timelines. The concept is *inclusive*, in that it brings in the military, corporate, academic, and civil sectors into the cycle, and *Small World*, in that it creates close interconnection. Above all, it is intended in peace time to get at the type of military advances and timelines only usually available in wartime. This is a means to better engage the grand and strategic with the operational and tactical.

Two key challenges are posed by Experimentation: first, persuading formal organizations to empower the process (when they may not see the need and, or, threat by doing otherwise) and second, creating a culture that learns from, adapts to, and anneals to failure—the testing of nulls, not just successes—*risk-taking rather than risk-averse*. It is by no means certain that the grand and strategic levels can be convinced—and they are unlikely to be so unless they see the advantage to themselves and not the operational and tactical levels attempting to control the grand and strategic, as per *Truppenführung*.

Returning to the Mulberry Docks and to Experimentation: why, for example, did one harbor fail and the other survive? Both harbors were identical and both placed adjacent to each other along the same piece of coastline—in fact the British Mulberry may have been the more exposed—and they both experienced the same storm on the 19th of June 1944. In hard traditional, thereby, measurable terms, there should have been no difference. Both should have failed or both succeeded. Yet one failed and the other did not. Something was clearly going on. Although conjecture, it is known that the Americans took less care in anchoring and placing their pontoons and docks, despite working from the same "song sheet." Why? Is it possible that the success of the one and the failure of the other had more to do with cultural differences? Could it be, as for the early oil exploration in the North Sea, that the Americans underestimated the hostility of the Channel and therefore they did not hear the same song of Charybdis? If Experimentation is to work, it will need to include these types of cultural and soft questions and seek to understand how they link across to the hard and technical values we are more used to dealing with, in order to create the type of networked effects we are looking for. This will require us to look again at the soft issues of Command balanced against the hard ones of Control.

One solution, attempted by the Soviet economies in the 20th century, was through commanding the different sectors (such as the economy), but which ended up trying to control them instead. Control in a military sense, or probably any other, has to be paid for in terms of time, rules, and bandwidth—and in achieving this type of end state, one loses the very advantages and fidelity provided by constructs such as *Truppenführung*—the end becomes the means. Ideally, one needs a balance between *Truppenführung* and *Führerprinzip*, the grand and strategic to the operational and tactical, Command to Control, and formal organizations to networks—and the point of balance may vary at different organizational levels. This new balance is likely to change the way we see ourselves and each other, what we say and how we understand, and will have cultural implications to the way we do our business. There may be experiences from which we can learn, but we may have little choice but to change—the context in which we are working is changing and, if formal organizations are to survive and networks to endure, a new relationship may be emerging.

CHAPTER 4

INFORMAL NETWORKS

Complexity ➡ Networks ➡

In this chapter, we want to consider what we mean by Informal Networks in an organization, how they form, what they are, and why they are valuable. From the management perspective, we also want to think about how such Informal Networks can be encouraged to form, and how they coexist with the formal management system.

WHAT IS AN INFORMAL NETWORK?

One answer is that it is a group of individuals in a company or organization that finds it mutually beneficial to stay connected to each other. It is a human, social interaction based on trust, shared values, and beliefs, and allows the sharing of information. This sharing in turn helps to build a shared understanding of issues important to the group. In such a network then, a node is a person, and a link is a bond or connection between two people, based on some level of mutual trust, which allows sharing of information. In a sense, this formality of definition then turns the Informal Network into something more formalized. These networks exist or develop in order to produce "action" where formal processes inhibit such channels.[68]

We can think of three levels of knowledge and information within such a social network.[69] Tacit knowledge is so deeply embedded in the individual that it is inexpressible. Implicit knowledge is embedded knowledge within mental models and beliefs that can be accessed and expressed. What is shared around the network is *information*. This information is then taken by an individual and given meaning within their individual context. Thus, even in a network where there is a high degree of mutual trust and extensive information sharing, each person will still have a different perspective on the key issues.

A key aspect of such networks is that they come together by mutual consent. No one imposes the membership of the network, or the links that are created. An important role for management is thus to create an environment in which such networks can thrive and have value. Managers have to learn in this case to "let go" of detailed control and to influence rather than direct the shape of the organization. To do this, they have to be convinced that such Informal Networks have value for the enterprise. Experience in the commercial world,[70] particularly from advertising and software development companies, indicates that this is most likely to happen in the following context:

---

[68] Verrall, "Exploring the Human Aspects of Information Management." see also: Gabriel et al., *Organizing and Organizations*.

[69] Verrall, ibid.

[70] CIO enterprise magazine. April 15, 1998. http://www.cio.com/archive/041598/index.html (May 2005)

When managers genuinely value relationships in the workplace, and truly listen to people and act on their suggestions, a culture of care and connection emerges in which people are highly responsive to the needs of the organization. Teams can form spontaneously and powerfully in this context, and the job gets done.

This quote does of course dodge the difficult issue of blending a team together from a number of disparate people (a process known as *team hardening*[71]).

A key aspect of such groups is that each individual in the group ideally becomes empowered—becomes a decisionmaker. Decisions are made by "us" not "them," although social dynamics such as group polarization and groupthink[72] can create barriers to such empowerment. We explore this duality a little bit further now. Who decides in an organization also depends on who learns, as we will see.

WHO DECIDES?

When the environment is stable (for example, the market for a product remains the same for a significant period of time, or the geopolitical context remains the same for a period, or the key management goal is to perform well-known tasks more and more efficiently), this leads to an emphasis on specialization, on defining boundaries, and on management by detailed instruction.

---

[71] Perry et al., "Exploring Information Superiority."

[72] Janis and Mann, *Decision-Making: A Psychological Analysis.*

The linear production line in the car industry is a clear example of a series of bounded and unchanging specializations that form part of a management by detail (micromanagement). This works wonderfully well provided that everyone wants a black Model T Ford. However, in today's and tomorrow's market environment, demand is more likely to include small batches of complex products, each with varied characteristics. In this much more variable and dynamic environment, the response has been to abandon the production line in some cases in favor of a number of very specialized cells that can self-organize in different ways through a process of mutual negotiation.[73]

In the same way, for an organization to thrive in a fast changing world, it has to allow such networking to flourish.

One way of looking at this is to consider how management style and the environment interact in terms of a two-by-two matrix (Figure 4.1).

On one axis of the matrix, we have plotted "Management Style," varying from "tightly coupled" to "loosely coupled." By tightly coupled, we mean management by detailed instruction—or Control, leading to a hierarchical management process. By loosely coupled, we mean the tolerance and encouragement of self-organizing Informal Networks of key individuals who share trust and knowledge—by Command. On the other axis, we have plotted the external environment ranging from "stable" to very dynamically varying and uncertain ("turbulent"). A tightly coupled management system succeeds when conditions are stable. In the defense context,

---

[73] Neubert et al., "Automated Negotiations." pp. 175-187.

Who decides?

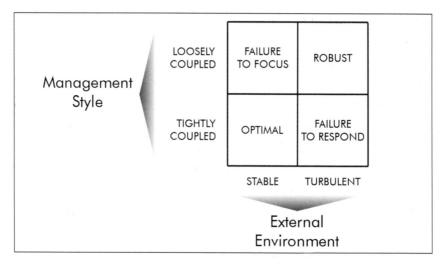

Figure 4.1: Management Style and the External Environment

the period of the Cold War was an example of awful stability—the threat stayed essentially constant for over 40 years. As a consequence, detailed roles and specialist forces were engineered, operating inside well-defined sectors of operations, and managed by an unchanging hierarchy of command. Operational research of this "scenario" went into more and more detail of particular pieces of the puzzle. A loosely coupled management process succeeds when conditions are very uncertain and dynamic. Again, relating to the defense context, multiple scenarios of the future now have to be considered, each with huge uncertainty associated with them. It is this uncertainty and a potentially very dynamic battlespace that is driving defense in the direction of "Edge Organizations"[74] that have the agility to cope. Operational research of these situations puts the emphasis on the spread of likely futures, rather than on the detail of a specific scenario.

---

[74] Alberts and Hayes, *Power to the Edge.*

Such a loosely coupled management process comes from the formal management structure "blessing" and encouraging the development of self-organizing networks within the enterprise. We have already seen some real examples of this in chapter 3, drawn from the defense context, where turbulence in the environment is real and failure to respond is severely punished.

CAN WE PROVE THAT INFORMAL NETWORKS ADD VALUE?

The cases we discussed earlier show that in those specific circumstances, a more loosely coupled management process really was necessary and really did work. However, we want to address here the issue of whether, from a more fundamental perspective, we can show that Informal Networks add value, and if so, how. One aspect worth bearing in mind during this discussion is that as roles within such an Informal Network develop, then the network itself in a sense becomes more formalized and enduring.

We start by revisiting some of the ideas of Complexity introduced in chapter 2, and expanded more fully in Moffat's *Complexity Theory.*[75] From these, the fundamental idea we need to introduce is that of *entropy*. Entropy, like energy, is a key property of all systems, including business or defense systems. Claude Shannon introduced a theory of information based on entropy[76] (that he called Information Entropy). So what is entropy, and why is it relevant here? Information Entropy is essentially a measure of uncertainty. It can also be related to the description length of a set of

---

[75] Moffat, *Complexity Theory and Network Centric Warfare.*
[76] Shannon, "A Mathematical Theory." pp. 370-423, 623-656.

data.[77] The shorter and more succinct the description is, the lower the Information Entropy is, and vice versa. A simple example helps to put this in some context.

A SIMPLE EXAMPLE

To understand this, we consider the management of a simple logistics system. This is a system providing fuel forward to frontline armed forces. In this context, we consider two U.K. Brigades engaged in a conflict (as was the case in the Gulf War of 1990-1991, for example). Each of these Brigades generates a demand for fuel as it maneuvers. If the logistics system is managed as a "push" process, where product is pushed forward based on a top-down plan of what is required, the management process looks like the left hand side of Figure 4.2 (based on Perry and Moffat[78]).

If the logistics system is led by demand, so that fuel is "pulled" forward based on the demand, then the picture is like the right hand side of the Figure. In practice, the actual system used will be a form of "directed" logistics, which falls between these extremes. However, we stick to these extremes to illustrate the issue. In the push case, there is just one decisionmaker (shown by the box shape), the Master, who decides on the basis of the plan who gets the next shipment forward. The extent of information sharing is shown by the dotted line in the Figure. In the push case, information is not shared—only the single decisionmaker has it and keeps it. Only he learns and adapts. In the pull case, information is shared across the network and all are empowered decisionmakers. All can learn and adapt. Mathe-

---

[77] Cover and Thomas, *Elements of Information Theory.*

[78] Perry and Moffat, *Information Sharing.*

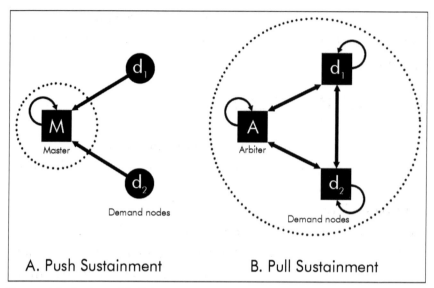

Figure 4.2: Push and Pull Logistics Systems

matically we can show[79] that the Information Entropy in the second case is significantly lower than in the first case. This means that more information is being shared around the network, leading to improved shared awareness. (We are ignoring here the effect of things such as information overload, which can have a counterbalancing effect, as discussed in depth in the RAND publication by Perry and Moffat.[80]) One key thing the mathematics indicates is that the sharing of information across such a network increases group shared awareness through the build up of correlations—in other words, increased understanding of how one thing relates to another. This corresponds to the common sense notion of an increase in understanding.

In the next part of this chapter, we want to explore the question of the types of Informal Networks that could arise in an organi-

---

[79] Perry and Moffat, *Information Sharing.*
[80] Ibid.

zation, and how different network structures can arise due to different formal management processes and different uses of technology for communication and interaction.

TYPES OF INFORMAL NETWORKS

There are three basic types of Informal Networks that have been the subject of systematic study. They were briefly introduced in chapter 2 because large networks of this type are examples of complex systems; they depend on significant local interaction between the large number of individuals in the network, and they can thus exhibit emergent behavior. We now delve into the properties of such complex networks more deeply, and look at some examples.

RANDOM NETWORKS

Random Networks form through individuals meeting up by accident rather than by design. A classic example is the creation of an informal group through meeting up at the coffee machine or water cooler. From the management perspective, such Random Networks can be encouraged by making people more accessible, and by making them move around. For example, in a typical office environment, people tend to stay in their offices. If they have a secretary, they are even more likely to stay isolated (either by accident or design). Many companies, including the HQ, U.K. Ministry of Defence, have abandoned this structure in favor of a more loosely coupled, open plan environment with coffee/tea points and break-out areas placed to encourage people to interact—although there are, perhaps, limits or extremes to its application in otherwise formal and hierarchical organizations where groups need to form across equivalent ranks, as well as between them. The type of social network that emerges from these interactions is a Random Network. The ease with which such links are formed is also, of course, a function of the personalities of the people involved and their willingness to change their behavior to accommodate the more free flowing work environment. Whether people can interact face to face in this way or whether they interact by phone or email changes the "psychological distance" between members of the network, and may make it harder to sustain.

More formally, we can define such a network as a set of nodes (the individuals) and a probability that any two individuals will interact. As noted already in chapter 2, one emergent property of such a network is that each individual has roughly the same number of links to others (this is called the degree). If we plot this on a graph we have Figure 4.3.

The peak of this plot is the mean number of links that each individual has with others, and the tails represent the scatter about this value, which reflects the randomness of the network.

Another key emergent property of Random Networks is that as we increase the probability of two individuals interacting, the network will suddenly undergo a change of phase, just like the water in chapter 2 suddenly exhibiting a different behavior as it is slowly heated, or water suddenly being able to percolate through a slab of rock.

This change of phase occurs suddenly rather than slowly, even though we increase the probability of interaction slowly. A small change in management support can thus cause a large-scale change in effect, which may not necessarily be by design or even secondary to the intended primary effect. In some instances, the advantage of achieving a primary effect

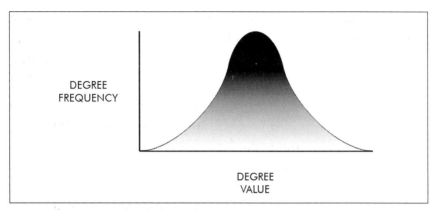

Figure 4.3: Degree distribution of a Random Network

can be outweighed by complex secondary and tertiary effects, which managers need to balance carefully before arriving at a decision.

SMALL WORLD NETWORKS

Small World Networks are so called because of the following phenomenon (again first discussed in chapter 2). Imagine that two people in the network are chosen at random, and then that the number of intermediate links between them is small (typically less than ten) even though there may be millions of people in the network. The classic example of this is the six degrees of separation effect discovered by Milgram.[81]

In this experiment, a target person was named and letters were sent out to random addresses in the U.S. The recipients were asked to pass this letter on to someone they knew well who might be closer to the target. On average, starting from the random "node," six links (i.e., six passings of the letter) were

---

[81] Milgram, "The Small World Problem." pp. 60-67.

sufficient to reach the target. Hence the phrase "six degrees of separation"—we are all (at least in the U.S.) just six links away from anyone else, via our acquaintance links. This is the Small World phenomenon. In addition to this, Small World Networks also exhibit another effect: high local clustering. This means that the neighbors of any node are well-linked to each other. We term this a high *clustering coefficient*. The key emergent properties of a Small World Network are thus the Small World Effect and a high clustering coefficient.

One way to generate a Small World Network (and the one we use here to define it in contrast to other types of networks) is to start with a number of isolated cells that are locally very well connected inside each cell, but have no connection between cells. We then generate a small number of shortcuts, random links that connect across cells. It turns out that you only need a very small number of shortcuts in order to turn this into a Small World Network.[82] From a management perspective, this is equivalent to encouraging local tightly knit cells of individuals to develop a few longer range contacts with people in other cells. The mathematics of the process[83] indicates that just a few of these are enough to produce the Small World Effect and high clustering coefficient required.

SCALE FREE NETWORKS

A Scale Free Network is characterized by the number of links an individual has to other members of the network. As introduced in chapter 2, we know that in a Scale Free Network, a few individuals are *hubs*. They have lots of links. However, most

---

[82] Watts, *Small Worlds*.

[83] Ibid.

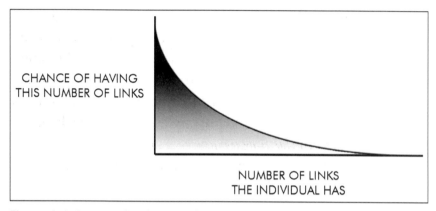

CHANCE OF HAVING
THIS NUMBER OF LINKS

NUMBER OF LINKS
THE INDIVIDUAL HAS

Figure 4.4: Degree distribution of a Scale Free Network

of the others only have a few links. This is very different from a Random Network, where everyone has roughly the same number of links. In fact, if we plot the number of links an individual has in a Scale Free Network versus the chance of having that number, it looks like Figure 4.4.

Because there is no defined peak value, this picture has no "scale" associated with it, hence the term Scale Free.

Again from chapter 2, we anticipate that Internet or Web-based links between individuals will tend to lead to Scale Free Networks. In a trawl of a large number of Web sites,[84] it was shown that with the Web sites as nodes, and hyperlinks between Web sites as the links, this forms a Scale Free Network. A similar trawl of a large number of Internet nodes showed that the physical Internet (with servers and routers as nodes and links) also forms a Scale Free Network.

[84] Albert and Barabasi, "Statistical Mechanics of Complex Networks."

It is possible to grow a Scale Free Network in the following way: Imagine you start with a small existing network of individuals, and a new person joins the team. If you encourage them to link with those who already are well-linked, then over time, with more arrivals, the network will tend towards a scale free structure. This is the "rich get richer" effect, where richness refers to the richness of connection of a person in the network. An apparently different mechanism that turns out to be equivalent is as follows: When a new node joins the network, this node connects, by two new links, to both node ends of a randomly chosen existing link of the network. This also generates a Scale Free Network.

COMPLEX NETWORKS AND FORMAL ORGANIZATIONS

In the early 19th century, economist David Ricardo theorized that organizations arrange themselves so as to maximize their competitive advantage, which, in historical times, tended to be about geo-political constraints. For example, the colder British Isles could not produce grapes in sufficient quantity (and quality) to satisfy the demand for fine wines. In order to satisfy their demand for wine, Britons had to sell something to the continent to produce a demand for their products not advantageously satisfied elsewhere. The solution to this dilemma was wool. From the basic need to supply an internal demand, international trade arose, which over time transformed the British landscape as landowners shifted to the production of wool and laborers, displaced by the agricultural shift, were employed to turn the wool into cloth. This process probably reached its apogee during the Highland Clearances of the 19th century, just as the Industrial Revolution was creating new competitive advantage in central and northern

The impetus for international commerce

England. And it was these same clearances that helped drive migration to the Americas and from the Anglo-Scots-Irish of the English-Scottish Borderlands (and Northern Ireland)—the Nixons, Clintons, Reagans, Bushes, and Washingtons amongst many—emerged the stock that formed the majority of U.S. Presidents. And, by the same complex turn of the screw, it was the arrival of the potato in Europe from the Americas that set in process the root causes of the single-crop potato famine of the 19th century that drove Irish immigration to the New World, and from which the Kennedys and Kerrys can trace their roots. Complexity in its truest form: over time creating not just new landscapes but new political philosophies as well, many of which can be traced back to wool and wine. The Lord Chancellor of the United Kingdom ceremonially sits on a highly decorated woolsack to this day!

The changing landscape of British trade and agriculture

The influence of the wool trade was not simply confined to Britain. On the western edge of Europe, it was to give rise to England's oldest alliance (going back to the 12th century) with another country: Portugal.[85] At the basis of this lay Britain's insatiable demand for trade, and after the Reformation and the change of Britain from Catholicism to Protestantism, this led even more frequently to disruption of its commerce with France, Spain, and thereby the New World. In Portugal, England found a partner that similarly feared Spain (the enemy of my enemy is my friend) and who had a demand for wool—if not for itself, then as an intermediary broker for the rest of Europe. Over the longer sea routes from Portugal to Britain, a new means of preserving (or fortifying) wine was

---

[85] In 1147, Afonso captured SantarÈm from the Moors, and, with the assistance of English and German crusaders bound for the Holy Land, he also captured Lisbon. In 1294, Afonso III's son Diniz (1279–1325) negotiated a commercial treaty with England.

required, from which arose Port. And Port is by no means the only wine that has been influenced by trade with Britain.

In the 18th century, French Huguenots fled France for Britain, bringing with them not just the silk trade that flourished until recently in the northwest of England around Manchester and in towns like Macclesfield, but also a love of fine wine and Champagne in particular. Champagne, as invented by Dom Perignon (by adding sugar to encourage a second fermentation and so bubbles), created a demand for wine from a region that, hitherto, had had little demand for its product. But there was a problem: the bottles kept exploding as pressure built up inside during the second fermentation process that takes place in the bottle itself. Huguenots arriving from Paris to England brought with them their love for fine things and the new ideas and loves of the Court and Parisians— including Champagne. This occurred at a time when Britain's Industrial Revolution was beginning to take place, and from which new forms of glass were emerging, including a dark-green, coal-based glass that could withstand much higher pressures. Glass from Britain, Champagne from France, and cork from the Mediterranean soon gave rise to a new three-way trade that continues to this day. It would be wrong to say that Britons invented both Port and Champagne, but perhaps to the chagrin of many Frenchmen, it would be right, equally, to say that both wines would not exist without the complex influence of others and of trade upon their development and production. The international center of the wine trade to this day is Britain, mostly because it continues to be unable to produce wine of any great quantity and quality and therefore must trade to import.

What has this got to do with Complexity, Formal and Informal Organizations, and Networks? Well, everything as it happens. If one looks at feudal Europe even up until the 18th century, a number of patterns emerge that overlap and intertwine. From a religious-political perspective, after the fall of Constantinople to Muslim-Ottoman troops under Mehmed the Conqueror in 1453, the center of Western Europe was Rome. It was Rome that anointed kings—or indeed excommunicated them—and it was Rome that arranged treaties between kings, enabling disputes to be settled and trade to flow. Individual kings might hold sway over their own fiefdoms, but outside these and across borders and seas, authority was vested in the writ of Holy Rome. Although the structures of Christendom emerged from the Roman Empire, normally taking on existing patterns and forms, over time these informal structures (networks) formed themselves into formal organizations—structured and authoritarian. These structures anointed kings and the kings anointed their courts, creating formal organizations for the dissipation of power and the accreditation of wealth, both material and spiritual. Rome and the Royal Courts over time became formal structures. The center of this Christian world was Rome and Rome created an authoritarian hub about which its formal organizations could exercise power.

But Rome could not succeed by Holy Writ alone and, within its remit, Small World Networks of clustered and interlinked cells—centered, more normally, along geo-political lines—emerged to satisfy the needs of the center. At the same time, more heretic, self-organizing, and Scale Free Networks also emerged about these hubs, with new adherents attracted to those already richly connected. These networks were not always against Rome, sometimes they were complementary and at other times—for example, in the period of the two

Popes (in Rome and France)—they created competition within the same organization. The point is that, much to the frustration of Rome, they existed alongside both the Church's "anointed" formal organizations and those Small World Networks it had blessed. Because these networks were not organized and controlled by Rome, they were in effect "rogue" or "heretic," even if they were largely influenced by Rome. One could not exist without the other: from the same complex structures that defined the writ of Rome emerged self-organizing networks that "tapped off its power" both in a complementary sense and in opposition. In simple terms, neither Rome nor its associated heretic networks could exist without the other.

During the period of the Inquisition, Holy Rome sought to track down these heretic networks that had arisen to challenge its power. Often this was a nonsensical and brutal witch hunt that sought confessions from innocent peoples under the threat of or actual duress. But, for the 300 years of its existence, the Inquisition (as distinct from the Spanish Inquisition that overlapped and succeeded the Inquisition), it also developed surprisingly sophisticated methods for dealing with the issue of rogue or heretic networks. For example, at an early stage, Inquisitors recognized that they needed to address certain elements of the heretic network: the go-betweens and gatekeepers between the rest of the world and the rogue network itself.

As ever, there were many foot soldiers, but for these soldiers to be resourced they required the go-betweens and gatekeepers to communicate with the rest of the world. Scale Free Networks also needed to be resourced if they were not just to survive but to pervade (persistence and growth over time). To pervade, they needed to continue spreading their network and feeding information and power back to the well-connected hubs about which they had formed: the rich get richer.

Rome had a choice (as Romualdo Pastor Satorras of the Polytechnic University of Catalonia and Alessandro Vespigniani of the International Center for Theoretical Physics in Trieste discovered, when looking at the spread of viruses): "they could immunize or remove 90 percent of the population to be effective," or "target the hubs" in the heretic social network. In order to stop the rich rogue network from getting richer, Rome had to target these hubs, their connections, and their ability to connect, essentially using its "gamekeepers" to police its networks. This was a much more efficient use of resources. By the end of the Inquisition, through trial and error; Inquisitors had determined that by getting at five to fifteen percent of these heretic hubs, they could "crash the system." The system would survive and persist (as networks tend to), but its pervasive virulence was disabled. For example, excommunication was used for the purpose of disabling otherwise hostile networks and needs to be understood for what it was: the denial of communication with Rome. Not just to be "out of communion" but to be cut off from the center of power. Although many English and Scottish Kings (including Robert the Bruce) ruled for periods of time excommunicated from Rome, in the end they all had to bow to Rome if they were to exercise legal authority and have access to the power of Rome. They could not exist or sustain a hereditary line outside the patronage of Rome. All roads (or connections) continued to lead to Rome.

In an informal sense, such self-organizing networks come into being to connect certain nodes to hubs of richly connected individuals blessed, perhaps, with certain skills or who, themselves, are anointed in some way to exercise power. Over time, if the hubs are to pervade then they need to exercise certain rules of behavior (for example, who can or cannot join the club and so be linked to the network). These rules also change the way that the hubs perform and behave and so how they relate to their associated network. This is not a chicken-or-egg question of which came first, the Scale Free Network or the Formal Organization? For as *Homo sapiens* man evolved, he did so in a scale free sense: clustering about certain groupings and individuals for specific reasons of sustenance, survival, and safety. As these clusters and associated networks and gatekeepers between different tribal communities grew, they came more and more in contact with each other. These communities (hubs and surrounding nodes), if they were not to be perpetually at war with each other, needed to find ways of working with each other—of maximizing their advantage and reducing hostile competition, wherever possible.

Recent analysis of the Y chromosome would suggest that women, in fact, travelled more widely than men during prehistorical times. This being the case, it appears most likely that women set the conditions for relationships between tribes and it was women who were crucial to determining exchanges between the different communities. To exercise this power, women needed to be close to the center of power. In other words, highly connected to a central hub or cluster, if not the hub or cluster itself. Men had less value; a man's need to be connected to the center was vested in his need to protect and nurture the central hub if his community was to survive and thus sustain him. In hard terms, men were expendable and could sustain themselves in isolation—the rogue male—from society and community, whereas women could not. These different skills persist to this day with the social linking skills of communication and language often being demonstrated more strongly amongst female populations, and spatial awareness and risk-taking more prevalent amongst males.

From these preconditions for survival, Scale Free Networks[86] began to evolve rules of conduct and behavior. As they evolved, these rules began to change the form of the original network. Hubs, if they were to pervade and to retain power, needed to do so in a more formal way; aggregating power to themselves, and controlling more formally their associated networks. In this way, the hubs, over time, evolved formal structures that needed and used rules of conduct and behavior in order to link with other organizations. Women were vital to this process, not only in determining the terms of trade between communities but providing credibility and value to the system. The rules that emerged protected and nurtured women, their community, and its relationships and trade with its neighbors.

As shown below, there is a complex interaction that continues to this day and is probably as much to do with evolutionary constructs as the context in which the rules are formed. Essentially, the self-organizing network is trust-based: individuals who join trust each other to do the right thing and are kinsmen or sufficiently related to the clan chief about whom they cluster not to require rules to determine how they aggregate and behave. They are, in effect, dis-aggregated and autonomous bodies linked through trusts and kinship. As these bodies grow, it becomes harder and harder for the network to arrange "trusted" linkages to others joining. Formal rules emerge in order to determine how these new bodies join and their relationships with others in the network and its hubs. These rules

---

[86] We assume that these self-organizing networks will tend to form by attraction to well-connected hubs, and hence will evolve into a scale free structure.

change the characteristics of the network. The hubs need to become more formal if they are to manage their connections to concentrate and dispense their power effectively. The network ceases to be self-organizing and scale free, and changes to being a network of formally defined locally clustered cells with longer range links between them: a Small World. As these new bodies form, some otherwise well-connected clusters are inevitably either disenfranchised or excluded from the new organization. If sufficiently well-connected, these disenfranchised or more loosely connected bodies may form new networks, splitting from the original network that formed them.

This returns in a roundabout way to the rule of "six degrees of separation" mentioned earlier. As organizations get larger, their "closeness" to the center extends. Within six handshakes of the President, the organization retains its presence and form. At the edge and beyond six handshakes, the trusts that bind the organization to its center start to dissipate until, inevitably, they begin to break. Closer hubs attract the outer or excluded elements of the network away from its center. In the past when communications were slow or hazardous, rules and trusts communicated from the center could frequently carry different meanings from those intended, or act so as to breach or break these trusts. The American Revolution, when placed in context, was fought initially not for a Republic but for reasons of home rule: "no taxation without representation." But, underlying the Revolution was the fact that the American colonies no longer felt within six handshakes of the King of England. Other attractors began to form around new leaders and hubs, such as Washington, who was as much interested in protecting his trade and commerce from the British taxman as he was in carving out a new state. It was also a close run thing, with many Loyalists fighting against the rebels, and the black population of the South, trusting not in Washington and the rebels to fight for their "freedom," but in Britain. What we saw, however, was a complicated political realignment, based upon the same judicial systems and, in place of the king, a president constrained by complicated checks and balances—formal organizations and their associated rules persisting to this day.

This evolution from initial self-organizing networks (which we assume to be scale free through the process of preferential attachment to well-connected hubs) to more structured communities of interest (forming Small World Networks because they represent locally clustered communities connected by "shortcuts") we call the Hypothesis of Network Evolution. It is shown schematically described in Figure 4.5, and it has the property of being potentially cyclical. Scale Free Networks develop around certain well-connected hubs. As these Scale Free Networks grow, they reach a point where they need to formalize their structures, to bless a King or Alpha cluster. In order to persist, the King or Alpha cluster has to "anoint" an organized and structured system, a Small World Network of clustered communities that will undertake his bidding. The Scale Free Network that anointed the King then has a number of choices. It can join the new network in order to retain its power source, thus forming itself into a Small World Network of interlinked, formally defined cells acting as a power grid for the dissipation of power; or it can fade away over time, no longer anointed by the King; or it can reform itself around new hubs in opposition or sympathetic to the original system.

Under certain conditions, in what is called a Bose-Einstein condensation, the network can collapse—as opposed to split—into a "star cluster" in which almost all nodes are linked to one

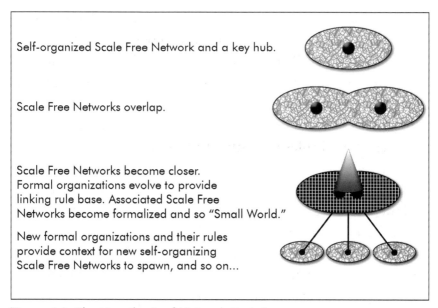

Self-organized Scale Free Network and a key hub.

Scale Free Networks overlap.

Scale Free Networks become closer.
Formal organizations evolve to provide
linking rule base. Associated Scale Free
Networks become formalized and so "Small World."

New formal organizations and their rules
provide context for new self-organizing
Scale Free Networks to spawn, and so on...

Figure 4.5: The Hypothesis of Network Evolution

dominant node. This happens particularly when nodes can be compared not just in terms of their richness, but also in terms of their fitness.[87] Fitness is an absolute measure of a node's attractiveness, which does not change with time, whereas richness changes as links are made to or taken away from a node. We can think of this in the following way. Consider the set of nodes of the existing network as a set of urns, with the number of balls in each urn corresponding to the degree of the node (the number links terminating at the node). A new node joins the network. The making of a link between the new node and the rest of the network adds a link to one of the existing nodes. This is thus the same as throwing a ball into the urn corresponding to that node. In wiring up the links from the new node to the set of existing nodes, we are thus throwing balls into a set of urns, with the chance of throwing the ball into a

---

[87] Albert and Barabasi, "Statistical Mechanics of Complex Networks."

particular urn proportional to the number of balls already in the urn. (We are assuming preferential attachment applies, so that the attraction of a node is proportional to the number of links it already possesses.) It can be shown that if we proceed in this way, the distribution of balls in the urns follows what is called a Bose-Einstein distribution, after the scientists Satyendra Nath Bose and Albert Einstein who jointly discovered it in relation to quantum mechanics. Any particular distribution of balls in the urns represents an outcome. Under Bose-Einstein statistics, all such outcomes have an equal probability of occurrence. We can see from this that the Bose-Einstein distribution explicitly allows for the possibility of most urns being nearly empty, and one urn containing most or all of the balls. This is a Bose-Einstein condensation.

In this state then, one hub or cluster becomes dominant to all other nodes in a dense, closely connected, almost homogeneous network. These types of condensed networks are very powerful, acting as a type of "black hole" to attract other nodes and networks into it. Because of their powerful attractiveness, they grow without the need for rules or formal organizations to set conditions or interpret them. A product completely dominating a particular market and causing all competitors to collapse is a possible example of such a condensation, where the network in this case links suppliers and customers (an example may be the market dominance of Microsoft).

Adam Smith, when he wrote of the invisible hand of capitalism, may have been referring in a sense to these types of star networks because they operate unseen, across boundaries and between people to determine the price—the real price—of a product and so set the conditions of how the market operates, and how a product comes to dominate the market. The Austrian economist Von Hayek also reflected this when he considered markets operating as information gatherers that come together to discover the price of a product and that there were good and bad rules: those that enabled the market to operate freely, or those that operated with a pre-determined outcome in mind. He suggested such pricing to represent a "spontaneous moment of equilibrium" formed from the influences of disequilibria that come together to determine a value or price. The British economist Ronald Coase took this further by suggesting that "factors of production need not be defined only in physical terms but also in the terms of the rights to act in a certain way."[88] Bad rules would inevitably set false and unsustainable prices; remove the rules and the value or price for that commodity would collapse.

In his article, "The Road from Serfdom: Foreseeing the Fall," Von Hayek wrote in the 1930s of the failure of the Soviet experiment. Without rules that encourage free markets to operate—to build trusts—powered by individuals wheeling and dealing in their own interest, he felt that it was not possible to coordinate the market. Authorities that attempted to over apply rules or to centralize them to meet their own pre-ordained outcomes distorted the market. The pricing mechanism, fundamental to the operating of the free market and upon which its trusts were built—and so the trusts between society and state—would fail. The state and its system would, over time, be seen to be operating illegitimately, denying its people their rights and the marketplace its values. The system was bound to fail. Fundamental to the marketplace and to exchanging values or prices are the trusts placed between the different players. If the market is not trusted, it cannot oper-

---

[88] Coase, "The Nature of the Firm: Influence." p. 22.

ate—there will be no true value. Networks operate in a similar fashion. They are built on trusts and the exchange of information. Self-organizing Scale Free Networks exist around certain well-placed nodes or hubs around which they link. Information is exchanged on a trust basis and the rich get richer, provided that the trusts remain. Organized Small World Networks based on a number of defined cells are aggregated in some way so that the hubs that get richer are identified formally. In Atkinson and Moffat's Hypothesis of Network Evolution, we postulate that hubs, over time, tend to operate as formal organizations, setting rules for joining the network and policing its membership. Where one does not have trusts, one needs rules. And rules are inherently inflexible, and time and space constrained. While they may set conditions, they do not have the fidelity and agility to enable the pricing mechanism to work—for the market to operate freely.

GETTING NEARER OR FURTHER?

In recent years many people have quoted the Peace of Westphalia in 1648 for its significance in providing the basis of three fundamental Western codes: the concept of the modern State, constructs of International Law, and our ideas of War and Peace, from which our notions for the division of religion and politics and Church from State persist to this day. But, as pointed out by Professor Shlomo Avatali writing in the Financial Times, underlying the Peace of Westphalia was a sectarian settlement between mainly Protestant northern Europe and the more Catholic south. The Peace of Westphalia was and became many things, but chiefly it was a recognition by Rome that it had to find ways of dealing with the heretical networks that were now existing successfully within their own formal organizations; networks outside its writ and, yet, with whom it was necessary to continue to communicate. In effect, the Inquisition also ended with the Peace of Westphalia.

We, in the West, take for granted now the codes that emerged from Westphalia without, perhaps, seeing the underlying requirements: the need to anoint and bless new networks that had emerged alongside the old code. Rome could no longer disable or prevent Protestant codes from emerging and was faced with the grim choice of either working alongside the new codes, and finding ways of dealing with them, or forever being in opposition. When we look today at the Muslim world, we should perhaps bear this in mind. During its first 900 years of successful expansion, Islam never needed to come to terms with an opposing sect or religion and, as a result, the codes and trusts between different states and sects, that we now take for granted, never formed. Islam has never been tempered by a collision of sufficient shock so as to change its ways of working from self-organizing to organized and rule-based.

As the late Ayatollah Khomeni remarked, "Religion is Politics or it is nothing," but this extends also to Western notions of the State and so to evolved state-based rules of behavior defined by International Law, and for which Islam has few parallels. New interactive connections need to form between the different systems from which ideas can be exchanged and trusts brokered. If they cannot, both sides will continue to feel threatened by the other, both unclear as to why they are under attack from the other.

Finally, there is no hard and fast analysis to determine which of the three main types of Informal Networks should be encouraged. In the defense context, the existence of cells of professionals dedicated to a specific task (such as anti-submarine warfare, for example) may well predispose such a network to be Small World in character, provided care is taken to put the necessary shortcuts in place. What is clear, however, is that both Informal Networks and the Formal Organizational structure are required to work well together in order to deliver the Agile Organization. And not only must they work well together, but they must also be able to work with each other and other forms of aggregation if they are to develop the type of trusts necessary to pervade, for which agility is key. We will show this in succeeding chapters, through a number of examples.

CHAPTER 5

SOCIAL LINKAGE AND DYNAMICS

Complexity ➡ Networks ➡ Effects

SOCIAL ORGANIZATIONS

So far, we have discussed the way in which organizations have to adapt and change in order to meet a rapidly changing environment. This has drawn on ideas from Complexity, Complex Adaptive Systems, and the emergence of complex social networks. Here we continue this line of thought by considering how such organizations and enterprises create effects and agility, and how these effects cascade through a network of influences in the external world. In order to do this, we first need to create a number of conceptual ideas and a language based on these, which we can then exploit in chapters 6 and 7.

Firstly, what is an "enterprise"? From the social perspective, we could define it to be a purposeful social collective. From a complex systems point of view, we could draw on ideas from chapter 2 and define it as an open system with energy and information flowing in and out across the boundary. From an economics perspective, we could define it as a networked set of autonomous (commercial) units whose transaction costs are lower if they cluster together.

What has changed is that, in moving from the Industrial Age to the Information Age, there has been a key shift in the way we organize commercial enterprises: from hierarchies to flatter, more empowered organizations; from organizing to *self-organizing* and self-synchronization.[89] The extent to which this is achievable depends inter alia on the institutional friction within the organization, a concept we revisit in chapter 7. In practice, such a culture change can take a long time to embed within the organization.

POLICY MAKING IN GOVERNMENT: A DEFENSE POLICY-RELATED EXAMPLE

Let us now consider in more detail what this shift means, moving from the commercial to the political and military context. At the highest level, some of the key factors are shown in Figure 5.1.

We consider, as shown in Figure 5.1, the higher level political and military process at the enterprise level in terms of a number of main drivers, shown by the boxes in Figure 5.1. We will now discuss some of these key drivers.

STAKEHOLDER PERCEPTION SPACE

The first is the stakeholder perception space. This consists of all political and military stakeholders (own, enemy, neutrals,

---

[89] Alberts and Hayes, *Power to the Edge.*

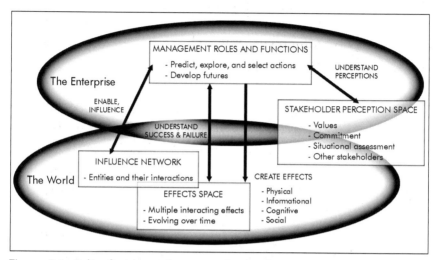

Figure 5.1: Policy factors at the enterprise level

non-government organizations, etc.). Some of these may lie within the enterprise, but most are outside in "The World" of Figure 5.1.[90] Each such stakeholder has his or her own internal values, commitment to particular objectives, a local perception of the situation, and hence a situation assessment, and interacts dynamically with the other stakeholders (e.g., forms coalitions, distrusts).

In order to discuss this process further, we need to consider how people interact with each other as part of this process. We conceive of this happening at a number of levels, although in practice the boundaries between these levels will be blurred. This draws from the work of Alberts and others in considering the implications of Network Centric Warfare.[91]

---

[90] Drawn from defense working group discussions on Command and Control, with acknowledgements to Anne-Marie Grisogono (DSTO, Australia) and Paul Phister (AFRL, USA).

[91] Alberts et al., *Understanding Information Age Warfare*.

Starting at the bottom layer, there is simple physical interaction (e.g., avoiding each other, or moving towards a common objective). Moving up to the next layer, we interact with each other by exchanging information (e.g., by talking face to face, by talking over the telephone, and by sending email). Moving up to the next level, we interact by creating and sharing a partially common understanding of a situation. At the top level, we interact by sharing (or otherwise) deeply held social values that bind us together or split us apart. This social context informs the whole process.

In summary terms, the physical domain is the physical world. The information domain is the space of all information sharing. The cognitive domain is the space where understanding develops. The social domain is where people share (or otherwise) more deeply held beliefs. History and culture, social and institutional structure, economics, and government and politics have most influence in the social domain.[92]

The stakeholders we have identified represent all those with a stake in the outcome. A central role of the enterprise is to attempt to *understand* and *influence* the perceptions and behaviors that drive the stakeholder community, as shown in Figure 5.1. This stakeholder perception space consists of at least four key attributes (residing in the social and cognitive domains) for each stakeholder, namely:

- Values and Trusts—the enduring values and trusts of the people involved;
- Commitment to Objectives—how committed people are to real achievements;

---

[92] Smith, *Effects Based Operations.*

Stakeholder perception space

- Current Situational Assessment—the perceptions people have of what is going on; and
- Predictive Situational Assessment—how things are likely to evolve from here.

This predictive situational assessment (how will things go from here?) will influence commitment to objectives, and these commitments will change over time. Current and/or past situational assessments will clearly influence predictive situational assessment in developing the perceptions of a number of likely "futures." Each of the stakeholders will have a support base within their own government, public, and/or media, and their chosen behaviors will be reflected in the influence network.

THE EFFECTS SPACE

Consider now the effects space of Figure 5.1. This represents the fact that the enterprise is seeking to create multiple effects in the physical, information, cognitive, and social domains of the other stakeholders, in the world outside the enterprise, creating perceptions, awareness, and shared awareness, which evolve over time as the situation unfolds.[93] The central role of the enterprise here is to understand these effects, and to discern which of these effects represent success or failure.

Effects descriptors or categories include the following:

- Degree of nonlinearity (how predictable/unpredictable are these futures?);
- Global versus local goals and effects; and

---

[93] For many examples of this see: Smith, *Effects Based Operations*.

- Actual predicted goals, wanted (aspirational) effects, and unwanted effects.

THE INFLUENCE NETWORK AND MANAGEMENT ROLES

In Figure 5.1, we have what we call the *influence network*, forming part of the world outside the enterprise. This represents the complex interplay of entities and their interactions, which allows an intervention to achieve an effect that moves the process in a positive direction. This influence network will be a Complex Adaptive System in general (as discussed in chapter 2), in which a particular stimulus will have a number of potential nonlinear cascading responses; there will not be just one effect, but an "effects cascade." The central role of management control here is to enable such interventions to achieve their desired consequences in effects space, enabling and influencing rather than directly controlling. Information will flow in across the boundary of this open, Complex Adaptive System, from information sources, stakeholders, world events, and the environment.

As an example of this cascade of effects, in chapter 2 we discussed in detail how the attack on Port Stanley airfield during the Falklands War of 1982 created an immediate effect in the physical domain (the disruption of takeoffs). This then cascaded to an effect in the cognitive and social domains through the realization (by the Argentineans) that airfields on the mainland might now be at risk of attack. This resulted in a move of the Argentinean Mirage fighters farther north (an effect in the physical domain), reducing escort fighter cover for attacks on the Royal Navy task force and reducing the pressure of these attacks. The Vulcan raids also boosted British morale before the difficult landings in San Carlos water (a cascaded effect in the social domain). The ultimate success of the task force bolstered Mrs. Thatcher's position at the political level (a cascaded political effect) in facing the Soviet Union during the Cold War.

In order to enable and influence this cascade of effects, management control at the enterprise level has to develop and predict futures. These capture how the world might be in stakeholder perception space under various assumptions. The management process then needs to be able to explore these futures, and from this exploration, select actions corresponding to setting initial conditions, or influencing the evolution of the entities and their interactions in the influence network.

For example, in the development of policy to counteract global terrorism (the "War on Terror"), the following may well come into play:

- **Understanding Perceptions**. Understanding the past and present perceptions of the stakeholders, their values, their current objectives and commitment to these objectives, and their current and predictive situational assessment.
- **Understanding the Influence Network**. Understanding the entities (actors, sensors, etc.), their interactions, and the flow of influence and causality. Understanding how the objectives, resources, authority, and constraints are propagated through the command system from the political to the actionable level.
- **Understanding Success and Failure**. Understanding political values and emergent centers of gravity (points of weakness).

- **Developing Futures**. Creating and exploring futures, estimating the consequences of interventions, and selecting a set of actions (a course of action).

This last point is based on the premise that we cannot predict the likely unfolding of future events. We can only estimate across a range of possible futures (none of which may in fact occur, of course).

All of the aspects above live at the socio-cognitive level of each of the stakeholders.

MANAGEMENT AGILITY: THE RANGE OF OPTIONS AVAILABLE

The range of actions available will be a function of the agility of the management system. This can be considered in the context of Cybernetics, as discussed in earlier times by Stafford Beer,[94] and we can think of it in the following way. We assume that the influence network of entities and their interactions have a certain complexity that we denote by the variety of the system. This is a measure of the number of different states or configurations that the system can find itself in, and hence is a measure of its *agility*. Ashby's Law of Requisite Variety from Cybernetics then requires that for this system to be in control, the variety of the controller (i.e., the management system) must match the variety of the system. Or, to put it another way,

---

[94] Beer, *The Heart of Enterprise.*

The larger the variety of actions available to a control system, the larger the variety of perturbations it is able to compensate.

—An Introduction to Cybernetics, Ashby, 1957[95]

And for *variety*, read *agility*. Agile management is required to control a dynamically agile system.

In Industrial Age management, we have, as a given, low agility of the management system due to its unlinked and hierarchical nature. To meet the requirements of Ashby's Law, we must then create low agility in the enterprise itself. This we do by partitioning into sectors, having specialized tasks that focus only on particular optimized roles and so on: a "stovepiped" organization. This produces the balance shown on the left-hand side of Figure 5.2, where low management agility matches low enterprise agility. The partitioning of the NATO forces in the central region of Europe into a "layer cake" structure of command during the Cold War period is a perfect example of this phenomenon. In the Information Age, with networked information sharing, we have a wider range of options available. This leads to better integrated, enterprise-wide, and more precise actions and effects. This corresponds to the right-hand side of Figure 5.2, where we have high management agility of the management system by design, matching the high agility of the complex and nonlinear influence network of entities (customers, stakeholders, and other enterprises) and their interactions. The challenge is to turn this desired agility into actuality.

---

[95] See also: Smith, *Effects Based Operations*.
Moffat, *Command and Control in the Information Age*.

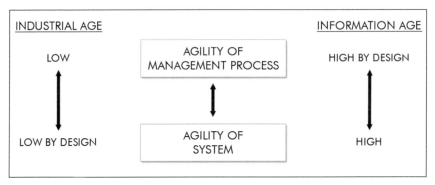

Figure 5.2: Ashby's Law of Requisite Variety and its implications for Information Age management and control

ENTERPRISE AGILITY AND INTEGRATION

Writers such as Kirkwood[96] have identified modern life as complex, intertwined, and networked, making the logical assessment of risk difficult. In a recent article discussing the implications of the Information Age for U.K. Defence Acquisition,[97] two factors were identified as important to achieving and maintaining integration at the defense enterprise level: "the level of intricacy of the enterprise (driven by the scale and complexity of the systems involved) and the rate of change needed to respond to changes in mission and technology (i.e., requirements and opportunities)." In other words, we can think of these as the complexity of the system of systems constituting the enterprise, and the agility of this system of systems in response to the rising uncertainty of possible missions and options.

Brook and Stevens then derive the picture in Figure 5.3 in terms of describing these key drivers of the system acquisition

---

[96] Kirkwood, "Why do we worry when scientists say there is no risk?" pp. 15-22.

[97] Brook and Stevens, "NEC: the implications for acquisition."

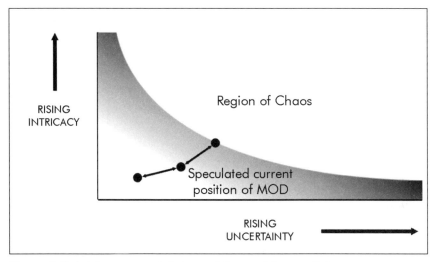

Figure 5.3: Intricacy, uncertainty, and the avoidance of chaos

process, and a speculated current position for the U.K. Ministry of Defence. There are two clear directions in which to go from here. One is a retreat back to the certainties of a more unlinked, less complex, and slower acquisition process. The other is an attempt to ride on the edge of chaos, exploiting the leverage that this might allow. The balance between these is delicate, in order to avoid entering the Region of Chaos.

Brook and Stevens point out that where intricacy and uncertainty are both high, the rate of change required of the acquisition system can be faster than the rate at which stable change can be delivered. As a result, the enterprise may become unstable when further change is applied, and we then indeed enter the Region of Chaos. These key drivers of Complexity are similar to the drivers identified by Smith[98] in creating chaos in the battlespace itself: the scale/scope of operations (c.f. Brook and Stevens: increasing scale and complexity, "intricacy") and

[98] Smith, *Effects Based Operations.*

the pace of operations (c.f. Brook and Stevens: increasing rate of change of mission and technology, "uncertainty").

DIRECTIVE AND EMERGENT MANAGEMENT AND CONTROL

We have already seen from Ashby's Law of Requisite Variety in Cybernetics how we can transition from centralized, directive management (the Industrial Age model) to decentralized, emergent management (the Information Age model). A key issue in any real organization is then the balance that is required between directive (centralized) management and control and emergent (decentralized) management and control of an enterprise.

Directive Planning consists of a rational assessment of alternatives based on a perceived understanding (i.e., an internal model) of how the underlying process operates. It is thus, in Cybernetic terms, feedforward control. In practice, of course, time horizons are bounded and information is imperfect, leading to a form of bounded rationality. An example in defense terms is the development of a campaign plan and "synchronization matrix," together with a number of contingency plans to take account of likely deviations between expectations and reality.

Emergent Planning is a much more immediate reaction to events as they arise—"stimulus and response." In defense force structure modelling, this approach conforms to Klein's Recognition Primed Decision Making (RPDM) psychological model of the decisionmaking process, applicable to expert decisionmakers under stress[99] working in fast-changing circumstances.

---

[99] Moffat, *Command and Control in the Information Age.*

DIRECTIVE VERSUS EMERGENT MANAGEMENT AND CONTROL

For a given situation or for a given style of management and control, there will be different mixtures of directive planning and management as opposed to emergent management. We can think of this as a control that is set at 1 for *directed* management and control, and set at 0 for *fully emergent* management and control. Within the enterprise structure, there will be a number of these controls at different levels and places in the process, all set at various values between 0 and 1, and whose settings will change with time and circumstances. This leads to a complex system that adapts over time as the situation changes.

Applying what we have learned of likely future defense force structures, and reading across to the commercial domain, we have the set of characteristics of the Information Age enterprise shown in Table 5.1, drawn directly from chapter 2.

Within this context, there is a creative tension between the overall intent of the organization and the local coevolution and synchronization of the local entities.

This tension is resolved at a particular level of the management process, and at a particular time, by the setting of the mix of directive versus emergent management and control. As already noted, the complex configuration of possible settings of the control at different levels and times is a significant contributor to the variety (and hence agility) of the management process.

Complexity Concept	Information Age Enterprise
Nonlinear interaction	The Enterprise is composed of a large number of nonlinearly interacting parts.
Decentralized control	There is no centralized management dictating the actions of each and every entity.
Self-organization	Local coevolution induces long-range order.
Non-equilibrium order	Interactions within the Enterprise proceed far from equilibrium. Correlation of local effects is key.
Coevolution	Entities must continually coevolve in a changing environment.
Collectivist dynamics	Cascades of local effects ripple through the Enterprise.

Table 5.1: The Relation between Complexity Concepts and the Information Age Enterprise

INFLUENCE NETWORKS AS COMPLEX SYSTEMS WITH EMERGENT BEHAVIOR

In order to understand the emergent behavior of the influence network, we need to develop some properties of networks that allow us to understand when they are essentially different from each other, and thus display different properties. We need to link network assumptions to network emergent behavior. This can be measured (building on ideas introduced in chapters 2 and 4) either statically, through the resultant *topology* of the network as measured by its degree distribution, average path length, or clustering coefficient for example, or through its *dynamics*, such as the growth and decay of nodes, the way in

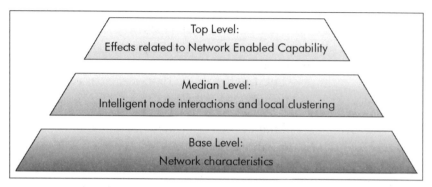

Figure 5.4: Classification of Complex Adaptive Networks at base, median, and top levels

which edges link up or break over time, and the sharing of attributes between nodes, resulting in clustering behavior.

This classification of such complex adaptive networks can apply at a number of levels, as shown in Figure 5.4. At the base level, we consider the basic node and linkage topology and dynamics of complex networks. At the median level, we consider the local interaction between (possibly intelligent) nodes, sharing a number of attributes of information, and the resultant clusters or cascades of the sharing of information that emerge across the network. At the top level, we consider how these feed through into Network Enabled Capability, located in the context of Complexity Theory as discussed by Moffat.[100] We start by considering what we call the base level.

---

[100] Moffat, *Complexity Theory and Network Centric Warfare.*

BASE LEVEL CLASSIFICATION OF NETWORK TYPES

It is clear[101] that a key classification property of a network at this base level is its distribution of degree, that is, the distribution of the number of edges per node of the network, which is a measure of the relative *richness* of node connections. In addition, it is possible to investigate the *average path length* (the mean number of edges between two randomly chosen nodes) and the *clustering coefficient* (a measure of how well-linked the neighbors of a given node are). All of these are useful measures of network connectivity, and lead to a first level classification of networks into the three main types: Random Networks, Small Worlds, and Scale Free Networks (see chapters 2 and 4).

Other characteristics of networks that can be investigated at this level are the *growth* of new nodes over time, and how these new nodes "plug in" to the existing network. For example, we can consider the *preference for attachment* of edges to nodes in terms of both node *fitness* and node *richness*, as discussed in chapter 4.

We also wish to consider the *vulnerability of the network to node or link loss* (in terms of the possible break up of the network into disconnected components that cannot communicate). We have seen that this can be radically different for each of the three categories of network we consider.

Finally, it is of interest to consider the number of loops there are in the network of a given length—a loop being a number of edges or links that start and finish at the same node. This is

---

[101] Albert and Barabasi, "Statistical Mechanics of Complex Networks."

another good measure of network structure. The number of such loops is determined by the adjacency matrix. This is the matrix of 0s and 1s corresponding to which node is attached to which. It turns out that the *spectral density* (i.e., the distribution of eigenvalues for the adjacency matrix) is directly related to the loop structure of the network.

CASCADING FAILURES
AT THE MEDIAN LEVEL

Moving up to the median level of Figure 5.4, we can consider more dynamic properties of the network such as how the removal of a node places additional strain on other nodes (due to load shedding in an electrical supply network, or information shedding in an information network, for example). This has been analyzed by Watts using the following network model. We assume that each node has a state that is either on or off, and that this state is determined by the states of neighbor nodes in the network. For example, the node is only on if a threshold fraction of neighbor nodes are on. In this model, the probability that a perturbation in an initially "all off" state can spread to the entire network can be connected to the existence of a "giant cluster" of vulnerable nodes. Watts[102] has shown for example that Scale Free Random Networks (i.e., Random Networks with a scale free degree distribution) are less vulnerable than normal Random Networks to such a perturbation. This approach to the modelling of complex networks has a clear connection to cellular automata models of complex systems such as the Bak-Sneppen evolution model of an adaptive ecosystem.[103]

---

[102] Watts. Santa Fe Working Paper 00-12-062.

[103] Moffat, *Complexity Theory and Network Centric Warfare.*

In Figure 5.4, we refer to the interaction of intelligent nodes and local clustering at the median level. An example in the defense domain of application is in the context of nodes that are decisionmakers (military commanders) linked across an information network. A cluster of such nodes corresponds to a set of such decisionmakers who agree to share the same critical information elements driving their decisionmaking, and who also agree to share and agree on the values of these information elements at any given point in time. The effects of such sharing can be measured using Information Entropy,[104] a concept introduced in chapter 4.

Having discussed how we can classify and understand such complex networks at the base and median levels of Figure 5.4, we turn in the next chapter to the challenging aspects of effects at the top level of our classification.

---

[104] Perry and Moffat, *Information Sharing Among Military Headquarters*.

CHAPTER 6

NEW ORDER: NEW EFFECTS

Complexity ➡ Networks ➡ Effects ➡

The end of our foundation is the knowledge of
causes, and secret motions of things; and the enlarging of the bounds of human empire, to the effecting
of all things possible.

—Francis Bacon, *New Atlantis*, 1627.

In this chapter, we explore in more depth the creation of
effects in the context of a "complex" adversary, and the consequences of this in terms of Command. We start by discussing
the nature of such effects in terms of what are called Effects
Based Operations.

The foundations of thinking behind Effects Based Operations
(EBO) were essentially laid down by COL John Warden USAF,
in the early 1990s. This followed his work on the strategy for
air power during the Gulf War of 1990-1991, based on analyzing the enemy as a number of "rings" of influence surrounding

the leadership. His concept was essentially one of multiple simultaneous effects, creating "shock and awe"[105] in the adversary system and leading to rapid collapse. This draws from the earlier thinking of Guilio Douhet and William Mitchell, whose ideas on the use of airpower led (inter alia) to the creation of the USAF as a separate force with strategic effect.

Over the past decade or so, thinking on EBO has evolved, and six theories or aspects of what this concept means have emerged.[106] These alternative views are set within the context of EBO as shaping and influencing behavior, as indicated in Figure 5.1 of chapter 5, where effects are created in the physical, information, cognitive, and social domains of the adversary. These then cause multiple and interacting effects to propagate over time in the "Effects Space" of Figure 5.1. In his discussion, Ho[107] recognizes that the breakthrough in thinking comes from understanding that "...every physical action has intermediate effects, also known as primary effects; secondary effects as well as tertiary and unintended effects, and treats the adversary as a Complex Adaptive System." This cascading of effects is the natural outcome of intervening in a complex system, as discussed in chapters 2 and 5.

THE SIX ASPECTS OF EFFECTS BASED OPERATIONS

1.   EBO is a method for planning an operation, which links the overall strategic goals to tasks to be under-

---

[105] A term first used in: Ullman and Wade, *Shock and Awe*.

[106] Ho, "The Advent of a New Way of War."

[107] Ho, ibid.

taken. The term *Effects Based Planning* has evolved to capture this concept.

2.   EBO is a method for analyzing alternative targets on the basis of the effect attacking such targets will have on the enemy, analyzed as a total interlinked and networked system. The term *Effects Based Targeting* captures this view.

3.   EBO is the application of all of the levers of national power, including the Diplomatic, Military, and Economic, to address all elements of the adversary's national power.

4.   EBO is the use of rapid, simultaneous, and parallel attacks in order to achieve the rapid collapse of the adversary system. We can capture this by the term *Shock and Awe*.

5.   EBO focuses on the interaction between the operational commander and other key actors in order to deal with a complex and adaptive adversary.

6.   EBO is a consideration of warfare as a clash between Complex Adaptive Systems, with nonlinear interactions between means and will, and the cascading of effects in the physical and psychological domains.[108]

The chain reactions of physical effects operate in a fashion analogous to falling dominoes. These domino chains may be relatively simple, or...they may be very complex in nature with many additional chains branching off...The relative predictability of the above physical chain reaction contrasts sharply with the chain of psychological and cognitive effects...The psychological chain, instead, is more analogous to a

---

[108] Smith, *Effects Based Operations.*

demonstration in which Ping-Pong balls are placed on spring-loaded mousetraps across the entire floor of a room, and are then set off by tossing a single ball into the room.[109]

In the U.K., our "Joint Vision" for future defense looks to realizing the full potential of the Maneuverist approach, exploiting the unexpected, using initiative and originality, and having the will to succeed. Effects Based Operations, creating effects across all dimensions of the strategic environment (economic, political, military, technological, socio-cultural, physical, legal, ethical, and moral), are seen as the best way of achieving this,[110] through the use of the Diplomatic, Military, and Economic levers of power.

In the rest of this chapter, we focus on one of the alternative theories of EBO in the context of informal networking to create a Complex Adaptive System with which to oppose the adversary's Complex Adaptive System (using the language of Smith[111]).

COMPLEXITY, EFFECTS, AND EXPERIMENTS

U.S. Transformation of its military forces encompasses three essential components: Network Centric Warfare[112] (NCW); Effects Based Operations[113] (EBO); and Experimentation.[114]

---

[109] Smith, *Effects Based Operations*.

[110] U.K. Ministry of Defence Paper. "Agile Command Capability."

[111] Smith, ibid.

[112] Alberts et al., *Network Centric Warfare*.

[113] Smith, ibid.

[114] Alberts et al., *Code of Best Practice for Experimentation*.

Given the *complex* nature of NCW and EBO, all three are interlinked, brought together and "proven" through Experimentation. Experimentation in U.K. terms may be understood as:

> Procedures undertaken to make a discovery, test a hypothesis, or determine a known fact—whose results and experiences from application are used to inform and base force development (transformation), concepts, training, education, acquisition, procurement, and policy decisions.[115]

As interpreted by both the U.K. MoD and the U.S. DoD, Experimentation is more of a campaign approach. It does not look at a single construct but many, and it does not confine itself to scientists and research staffs. It is complementary to, not in competition with, Operational Research studies of the issues. The concept is essentially cyclical; to be successful it will need to place scientists and industrialists in the front line as much as it places military and civil service staffs alongside their counterparts in industry and research laboratories. Its harnessing of "revolutionary advances in the technology of war"[116] and placing of concepts, systems, and processes more rapidly into the battlespace than hitherto has been possible will be a mark of its success; in effect, by capturing grand strategic policies and testing these across the strategic, operational, and tactical domains—against new and emerging technologies in partnership with the industrial-military economy—to leverage technological advantage in the battlespace. Fundamentally, Experimentation should be about testing Complexity and the

---

[115] Broadly introduced by the "MoD Defence Strategic Guidance, 2003."

[116] President George W. Bush, speaking on U.S. Transformation, 2002.

many Complex Adaptive Systems that aggregate to form the battlespace. It is not a single, linear, or simple testing of one or more similar products in different venues, but the testing of an idea in an unbiased "context necessary for success" against an underlying (innovative) hypothesis using reliable and observable metrics that reduce the risks and uncertainties and provide "unambiguous evidence of what has been observed" emerging across "relevant sets of operators, researchers and decision-makers."[117] Crucially, Experimentation attempts to model the very Complex Adaptive Systems that underpin both Network Centric Warfare and Effects Based Operations.

Although both the U.K. and the U.S. agree on the essential component parts and constructs for NCW, EBO, and Experimentation, and are working to realize these new ways of aggregation, there are key differences as to why each nation has arrived at this position and how the constructs will be interpreted. Funding for the four U.S. services—the U.S. Navy, the U.S. Marine Corps, the U.S. Army, and the U.S. Air Force—is through separate "Title 10" funding, unlike the joint funding for British forces: the Royal Navy (including the Royal Marines), the British Army, and the Royal Air Force. U.S. forces are therefore aggregated along single service lines until they are made joint— a type of top-down approach. Whereas, U.K. forces are organized along single service lines but jointly aggregated—more bottom-up. There is no right answer, but given the same *inputs* one might see different *outputs* while achieving the same *outcomes*. Economically, the U.K. military budget acts akin to the Euro by providing a *single currency* for all three services, while the four U.S. services effectively preserve their own single-service currencies. The *single military pound* has to pay for all three U.K. services and

---

[117] Alberts et al., *Code of Best Practice for Experimentation.* pp. 38-39.

its supporting civil service. Inefficiency in any one part of the military economy needs to be paid for elsewhere from within the same budget. For example, an inefficient aggregation of Army resources about, say, Divisional and Corps structures, would have to be paid for in terms of fewer ships, aircraft, tanks and headquarter staffs, whereas the U.S. Army can do so largely at its own expense (albeit at the expense of the overall effectiveness of U.S. armed forces) and not that of the other services. Interactivity between the four U.S. services therefore occurs at a higher level than in the U.K., essentially at the grand and strategic levels as opposed to the operational and tactical. In an economic sense, the U.S. military economy (at between 7 to 10 times the size of the equivalent U.K. military economy) acts very much like the U.S. dollar as a type of "prime currency," largely immune to the forces affecting smaller and secondary currencies, such as the pound. Consequently, the four separate U.S. military currencies operating within the combined U.S. military economy can afford to pursue inflationary or inefficient policies that would cripple the British military economy. In practical terms, this means that, while the U.S. military economy might choose to run a number of different projects against each other, if necessary in all four services, and then select the best solution for each domain, the U.K. military economy cannot afford such a choice. It must set its "interest" rates appropriately in order to maintain balance with the U.S. military economy while preserving "demand" on its products, at an affordable rate. A low pound (high inflation: low interest) means that the U.K. sells more abroad but cannot afford to buy/influence[118] as much, while a high pound (low inflation: high interest) means that the

---

[118] Taken to mean "the strategic effect a person or thing has on another in the exercising and flow of moral ascendancy to affect character and destiny."

U.K. cannot sell as much abroad but we can afford to buy/influence much more.

The degree of scale therefore matters, but the way that the two military economies are scaled is also significant. This is a complex national military-industrial[119] economy that must be balanced against other demands within the (international) political economy while responding "to changes in mission and technology (i.e., requirements and opportunities)."[120] Unable politically, constitutionally, and so economically to change the aggregation of U.S. forces at the operational and tactical levels along joint lines, the DoD has sought to create joint structures at the strategic level where the four single services can be brought together. U.S. Transformation in this regard is about "jointery" in U.K. terms—a move towards a more efficient and relevant aggregation of military force away from the straightjacket imposed by Title 10 expenditure. Its core tenet is to form new and more flexible networked force structures from across the four U.S. services: the USN, the USMC, the USA, and the USAF. Thus, in U.S. terms, Transformation is about the *network* and making the single services more interactive; it is about creating these new forms aggregated about or *centric* to the DoD (as opposed to the single service chiefs); and so creating more joint and efficient means of *warfare*. *Network Centric Warfare* in this regard means exactly what it says and, ultimately, this is about breaking down the single-service stovepipes at the grand and strategic levels.

---

[119] President Dwight D. Eisenhower, "Military-Industrial Complex Speech," last "good night" speech as President, 1961.

[120] Brook and Stevens, "NEC: the implications for acquisition." (first mentioned in Chapter 5).

Complexity, effects, and experiments

The Lockheed Martin X-35 Joint Strike Fighter, designed to support all military services in multiple combat roles

Without the degree of joint interactivity at the lower operational and tactical levels creating demands on the strategic and grand-strategic levels, U.S. forces need "jointery" at the higher levels. Thus, in *scaled* terms, the U.S. and the U.K. military forces are aggregated very differently. For the same reasons of leveraging "power to the edge" and realizing information superiority, the U.K. has embarked upon a similar transformation or development of its forces. But, being more joint already and funded as such, this has translated into forming new and more efficient *networks* across the joint domains in order to *enable* and so leverage greater *capability* from existing resources (hence *Network Enabled Capability: NEC*). Consequently, although the inputs are the same—both the U.S. and the U.K. are attempting to move their military from the *Industrial* towards the *Information Age* and towards a new form of "military information complex"—the *outputs* (in terms of the aggregation of forces) may be different, even although the *outcomes* (in terms of improved force effectiveness) may be the same.

EFFECTING ALL THINGS POSSIBLE

The effectiveness of the Kosovo Air Campaign of 1999 was not judged a success. The Former Yugoslav Army remained largely intact despite an intense air assault aimed against it, and the campaign failed to achieve its political intent. From this, and from the earlier thinking on Effects Based Operations, arose a requirement for improved levels of targeting to achieve desired political—as opposed to just a military—end state. As a result, the U.S. Air Force, as supported by the U.S. Navy and the Royal Navy and Royal Air Force, led on *Effects Based Targeting.* Initially confined to the air campaign, increasingly it was recognized by military planners that to achieve the political end state meant not just affecting the military but also the economic and diplomatic resources available to the enemy. One domain in isolation could not create the desired effect: the air campaign alone in Kosovo did not *coerce* Serbia or cause the withdrawal of its forces. This, in turn, led to a re-examination in both the U.S. and the U.K. as to how the different departments of state might interact to create desired effects across the *complex* (joint and coalition) military, economic, and diplomatic domains.[121]

One of the key aspects of Effects Based Operations is the development of linkages and *interactivity* between the different departments of state to enable cognitive reasoning by key decisionmakers. This linking across the required levels creates a

---

[121] The U.S. considers the Diplomatic, Information, Military, and Economic (DIME) levers of power, whereas for reasons of political sensitivities, the U.K. considers the Diplomatic, Military, and Economic (DME) levers of power.

Complex Adaptive System to oppose the Complex Adaptive System that is the adversary. But just as the U.S. and U.K. military are *aggregated* differently, so too are the different departments of state. In the U.K., most departments of state do not have the same asset base and planning departments that are vested in the MoD. In military terms, they operate more at the grand and strategic levels than they do at the operational and tactical. The temporal context in which grand to tactical policies operate is at two levels. The first is within the politically driven policy cycle of about 2 years within a 4 to 5 year parliamentary term;[122] the second is in the far, medium, and near terms. Broadly, grand strategic and strategic policy is expected to look forward 16 to 20 years; strategic-operational policy 6 to 15 years; operational-tactical 1 to 5 years; and the tactical from the immediate out to 12 months.

Clearly there are overlaps; each policy level influences the other, each interlinked and *networked* across to the other. The armed forces in most developed states, uniquely amongst other government departments, are configured to occupy each of the different policy levels looking across the different *complex* temporal domains. So, at the tactical levels exist the different deployed units; at the operational level the unit and front line commands, logisticians and support bases; at the strategic level, the single service, joint chiefs, and defense procurers/suppliers; and at the grand level, ministers and senior policy makers—combining *practitioners* through to *planners*.

Few other Ministries are as well served—the Home Office does not directly "own" the different police constabularies; the

---

[122] This is the same in the U.S. as it is in the U.K., Sweden, and Australia.

Treasury does not run its own local banks nor, now, the Bank of England, and the Foreign and Commonwealth Office does not directly control development funding and investment. In one area the different entities do come together: intelligence. But, until recently,[123] this too has been divided strictly between MI5 (the Home Office), MI6 (the Foreign and Commonwealth Office), and the Defence Intelligence Service (DIS).

In the first few years of the 21st century, there were important examples of single-issue adaptive networks challenging governments. The Fuel Strike organized by a number of determined individuals protesting at the price of fuel, informally networked across the Internet and using mobile phones, almost brought the British economy to a halt in 2000. Able to blockade the few-in-number but highly efficient oil terminals and to influence the tanker drivers responsible for delivering fuel across the country, protesters "turned off the tap" within days. In terms understood by Effects Based Operations, a small number of highly networked and interactive individuals had created an economic *effect* in order to leverage a political response. Using the *resources* at their disposal, they had taken *action* to influence the different oil terminals (*nodes*) to achieve a desired *effect*. The Chancellor agreed to look at their grievances. The protesters in question, aggregated at the tactical and operational levels, had used the principles of *Truppenführung*[124] to achieve their desired grand strategic and strategic *effect*.

---

[123] One of the results falling out from 9/11 and the need to better interlink the different intelligence agencies has been the formation of thematic "joint" intelligence centers—combining all three sources of intelligence, their different cultures, and "outlooks."

[124] Truppenführung: troop leadership or unit command.

The following February, Foot and Mouth, a highly communicable and thereby networkable disease, infected the national cattle and sheep herds in England, Wales, and Scotland. Again, resourced and interactive at the grand and strategic levels, the then Ministry of Agriculture, Food, and Fish proved incapable of stopping its spread. Although a notifiable disease, lack of adequate controls and inspections exacerbated by poor food and animal husbandry standards had allowed the disease a 2-week head start. Unable initially to address the issue effectively at the operational and tactical levels—where the disease needed to be tackled—the department wasted time attempting to understand the issues rather than mobilizing resources (vets and local councils) to their cause. By the time effective action began to be taken, it was too late for many flocks, although the policy decisions made (supported by Operational Research) did bring the problem under control.

In Cumbria, there were one or two successes. By galvanising public reaction across the Alston Moor, the local vets, Mr. and Mrs. Jim Clapp, were able to protect the wethered[125] flock local to the region by using preventative measure against the spread of Foot and Mouth to the High Pennines. And in the Lake District and parts of Cornwall and Devon, the armed forces (again supported by Operational Research) provided the operational and tactical planning and resources necessary to tackle the disease. Initially, Councils had attempted to use the armed forces as logistical support only—digging graves and ferrying carcases. But, quickly the forces brought to bear their tactical and operational planning skills, successfully establishing local networks across the dif-

---

[125] Whethered sheep are those sheep that over generations have built up an understanding and likeness specific to their valley or region.

ferent organizations and fighting the disease at the corporal level, where command was effectively vested. Corporals and junior officers were *delegated strategic authority* to place operational contracts and to direct diggers and transport on behalf of the local council and government to create the desired *tactical* and thereby *strategic effect*.

The communicable disease SARS may also have demonstrated similar challenges to more *institutional* forms of government at the grand and strategic levels. Identified first in Hong Kong, where arguably "candid policy debates" across the different professions are still permitted, it proved "too risky (in China from where the disease had originated) for elites to act solely on their ideological convictions and policy concerns"[126] and where it took the Chinese President to intervene, personally, before effective action was taken.

Effects Based Operations are therefore enabled by creating highly interactive and so Complex Adaptive Systems and networks, not just across the different grand to tactical (temporal) levels of government, but also between and across departments. Crucially, grand and strategic policies need to set a broader vision and future context in which the operational and tactical levels can trust, aim for, and work towards. Without this broader context, the tactical and operational levels have nothing to aim at—the essential coherence between the near and the far is lost.[127] There are issues that flow from this: first, the grand and strategic institutes need to create the broader rules setting out their future visions and, secondly, they need to bless the different

---

[126] Zhu, *Gun Barrel Politics*. p. 229.

[127] "Man shall not live by bread alone, but by every word that proceedeth out of the mouth of God." St Matthew ch.4, v.7. See also Deuteronomy ch.6, v.16.

strategic to tactical networks to implement their visions. At the tactical and operational levels, too, one needs *rule bases*—the institutes formed around and within regiments, ships, aircraft, and command staffs to secure the grand strategic vision while enforcing the "strict legal and procedural protection, without which"[128] the networks and systems necessary to realize adaptively a future complex context simply cannot exist.

Nazi Germany did not fail at the tactical and operational levels; it failed because it was unable to offer more to its people and the people of Europe than war and continued struggle. As a result, it was unable to exploit the tactical and operational advantages brought it by *Truppenführung* and *Führerprinzip* at the grand strategic level. But there are other examples closer to home. Despite better trained and equipped soldiers and sailors and winning almost every set piece battle, Britain failed to win the War of Independence. It simply did not have an alternative grand and strategic vision to offer its own soldiers, fighting and dying for the Empire, or their Loyalist supporters. The Republicans, by contrast, created a believable grand and strategic vision, which over time prevailed operationally and tactically. For many years, the perceived wisdom for the failure of the U.S. in Vietnam was that there had been too much political interference, and that the U.S. Army lost because of it. Eliot A. Cohen refutes this.[129] It is his opinion that the U.S. lost Vietnam because the politicians were too *little* involved—they failed from 1964 onwards to provide the type of grand and strategic vision that could be *trusted* by the Vietnamese, the U.S. soldiers fighting there, and most significantly, the American public watching a contrary tactical vision (the body count) unfold before them.

---

[128] Zhu, *Gun Barrel Politics*. p. 229.

[129] Cohen, *Supreme Command*.

Effects Basing and NCW/NEC are therefore inextricably linked. Given the complex and adaptive nature of the two constructs, and the systems within which they need to apply and be applied, a new means of integrated testing was required. This has found expression with Experimentation.

THAT HE SHOULD NOT BE ABLE TO COMMAND THE RAIN[130]

Command and Control in its broadest sense may be considered as a means of aggregating and dispersing power. At its simplest, control may be considered as something *exerted on* another person, or a *system to direct, rule,* or *regulate,* as required: "those structures and processes devised by command to manage risk,"[131] whereas command is more about *guidance,* an outward expression of *desired* (rather than directed) *intent:* "The creative expression of human will necessary to accomplish a mission."[132] The two are not synonymous and yet in recent years have come to be seen as such. Historically, the two terms first appear to have come together during the conflict between President Truman and General MacArthur during the Korean War, when MacArthur effectively challenged the President's "grand and strategic command (as Commander in Chief)"[133] through his "operational control" of U.S. and U.N. forces. MacArthur's underestimation of Chinese forces and

---

[130] "But methought it lessened my esteem of a king, that he should not be able to command the rain." Samuel Pepys. Diary, 19 July 1662.

[131] McCann and Pigeau, "Clarifying the Concepts of Command and Control."

[132] Ibid.

[133] The phrase "Commander-in-Chief" had existed in British law since 1639 when King Charles the First appointed a "Commander-in-Chief" over the English Army fighting in the First Bishop's War, just prior to the Civil Wars of England, Ireland, and Scotland.

the concerns expressed by both the British and French governments as to his handling of the war gave Truman the authority and confidence to exert his constitutional rights and so remove MacArthur. This did, however, give rise to the concept of Command and Control and a view that they subsequently came for many years to mean one and the same thing—as linked by the acronym C2. In the subsequent generations, the term has been further enhanced, expanded and misused to include C3 (Command, Control and Communications) and C4ISR (Command, Control, Communications and Computers, Information, Surveillance, and Reconnaissance). At each iteration, the essential meaning and difference between the two has been lost, with each addition being more about the technical delivery of tactical and operational control than an expression of command: "the root tenets of command and control are timeless, but they have been lost in the chase for new technologies."[134]

The aggregation and dispersal of power within a highly networked and distributive organization is fundamental to its behavior. A Complex Adaptive System, by its nature, is reliant upon the many different interactions that aggregate to constitute and define it: its *outputs* and *outcomes*. These interactions are essentially asynchronous (see chapter 2); they are not and cannot be controlled, and yet can combine to synchronous[135] effect. Taken to its logical conclusion, the behavior of Complex Adaptive Systems cannot be controlled; they can only be influenced and bounded (as discussed in chapter 5), which poses a

---

[134] Vice Admiral Robert F. Willard, U.S. Navy, writing in "Proceedings." October 2002.

[135] Taken to mean: "the affect formed by the simultaneous occurrence of related normally asynchronous events to cause meaningful effect."

That he should not be able to command the rain

problem to planning staffs wishing to create effects that apply structured rule bases in accordance with policy directives.

From this perspective, Effects Based Planning deals essentially with systems that are themselves highly interactive and networked—the Influence Networks of chapter 5. To achieve the desired effect on another system therefore requires a detailed understanding of "one's own systems" and how they in turn interact with those of "the other." Advances in communications and globalization have linked the Diplomatic (, Information), Military, and Economic domains of friend and foe as never before—themselves under the close scrutiny of the U.N., International Law, and the media. Moreover, in terms of Just War,[136] the use of force must be proportionate and discriminate, thus, although a first order effect may gain just advantage, if the second and third order effects are *disproportionate* and/or *indiscriminate*, these may outweigh any advantage; the action may be *unjust* and potentially, thereby, illegal.

Wars fought previously in remote unconnected locations, beyond the immediate purview of accountable politicians and the world's media, could be fought on a largely autonomous basis. A commander could be given his marching or sealed orders by his Commander-in-Chief and allowed to prosecute the war with little direct interference unless he required more resources or seemed to be losing. In the 20th century this all changed, as wars connected in a more complex Clausewitzean manner the military and the civil with political goals. By the 21st century, globalization meant that

---

[136] Just War Theory (JWT) as now understood, like International Law, traces its lineage through the 30 Year War (1618-1648) to the Peace of Westphalia, and specifically the great work of Hugo Grotius, De Jure Belli ac Pacis (The Law of War and Peace), published in 1625.

That he should not be able to command the rain

every state and person is also *connected* directly—no matter how weakly—to "the other." The peace or *pax* became linked inextricably and connected to the peace of others. Yet many commanders remained convinced that political control over their "command" was to be resisted; many citing failure in Vietnam as an example of excessive political control.[137] Effects Basing therefore, while allowing commanders[138] the potential to exercise more effective tactical and operational command (by connecting across the levers of power), comes at the price of enabling and delivering grand and strategic objectives in furtherance of political aims—potentially a form of directed control.[139]

This returns to the balance of command with control and how these are aggregated appropriately to the Information Age. A different way of looking at Command and Control is to consider that Command and Control interact with each other— that one man's command is another's control. In this respect, command may be seen as a centrifugal force (outward); whereas control is centripetal (inward). If this were the case, the system described would effectively be an open loop: commands would be passed down the chain with no interaction between those being controlled and those commanded. In a hierarchical, more institutional, industrial and thereby *rule-based* organization, this can occur with little interactive feedback to command. Given the type of Complex Adaptive Systems and highly interactive and networked commands (based upon the

---

[137] As refuted by Cohen, *Supreme Command*.

[138] "Commanders must learn to specify what they want to do, not what they want to own, and what they want to do with it." Keynote address to the IQPC conference by Vice Admiral Sir Jeremy Blackham, then Deputy Chief of Defence Staff (Equipment Capability). 27 May 2002.

[139] "Who can control his fate?" Shakespeare. *Othello*. Act V, Scene 2, line 304.

That he should not be able to command the rain

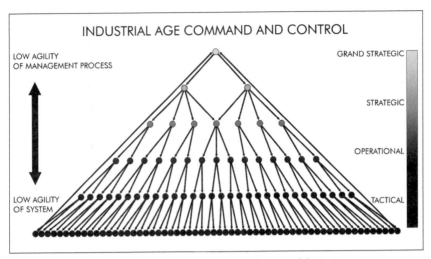

Figure 6.1: Industrial Age Management applying Ashby's Law

application of information to leverage Knowledge Advantage and Decision Superiority[140]), required to be understood, applied and influenced by Effects Basing, this type of industrial control is no longer applicable.

Ashby's Law of Requisite Variety is introduced in chapter 5 in the context of Industrial and Information Age management and control. From this perspective, the "open loop" Command and Control system typical of the Industrial Age is shown above in Figure 6.1. Each person in the chain was rigidly controlled within a tightly applied stovepipe and delivered an *output* as required by the *input*. There was little or no lateral movement—each function could be undertaken within the guidelines provided. In terms of mass production, tightly controlled about hard and thereby quantitative metrics, the above system effectively produced mass or quantitative *outcomes*. The

---

[140] Taken to mean "the exercise or instance of resolving, judging, and so concluding on actions, affects, persons, or things more advantageously."

That he should not be able to command the rain

system worked as long as *outcomes* might be judged on the attritional basis of "mass on mass."[141] It broke down as soon as the *controlled* guidelines by which mass was managed were challenged. If assembly workers did not receive what they were expecting, the whole production line came to a halt; they were not empowered to look for alternatives. Similarly, the assembly-worker could not change the nature of the product to reflect a more qualitative requirement; instead he had to await orders or "dangerously" represent change upwards. Both the management process and the design of the system had little or no agility to allow for changes to inputs, outputs, or outcomes.

The grand and strategic overview of the organization was provided by only a limited number of senior managers who had to get the direction right if the rest of the organization was to survive. The lower operational and tactical levels were absolutely reliant upon direction from above if they were to maintain their jobs, and interaction across the levels was rarely encouraged. Provided that the product in some way matched the grand and strategic aspirations of the marketplace—there was sufficient demand—the system held good. But the organization also polarized working practices: senior managers tended to be cerebrally overloaded and physically under loaded whereas it was the reverse for their juniors. For as long as the tactical and operational nature of the marketplace determined decision-making, the industrial system could cope, but as soon as more complex and less linear requirements were placed on the system (at any level), it began to break down. Managers did not have the *fidelity of command* to sense and so make the changes necessary to match output to outcomes. In response to agility,

---

[141] Attrition warfare is the placing of your strength against his strength. Maneuver warfare is the placing of your strength against his weakness. (From a discussion with General Sir Rupert Smith, former DSACEUR)

That he should not be able to command the rain

the marketplace created many different companies, producing essentially the same product, using mass to provide qualitative choice: "Quantity has a Quality all of its Own."[142]

To illuminate this point, it can be hypothesized that the BEF went to fight a war in 1939 based on industrial and controlled lines: *Befehlstaktik*. The German Army, when it swept through France in 1940, employed the tactics of *Auftragstaktik* and *Truppenführung* agilely to achieve Knowledge Advantage and Decision Superiority, from which it leveraged grand and strategic effect at the operational and tactical levels. Unable to respond effectively in the time available, or to shore up and buy time for the collapsing French Army (as it had been able to do in 1914), its maneuver counter-offensive at Arras was the exception. Despite strategic advantage and a concentrated preponderance of manpower, intelligence, and equipment (mass), the British Army was out-fought and, more crucially, "outthought." Strategic command crumbled and operational/tactical control failed. There was not the agility or fidelity to respond. It could no longer use mass to make up for qualitative[143] shortcomings as it had done in the First World War, as late as the spring of 1918.

The industrial system held good for so long as control could be exercised along timely, linear "mass on mass" or attritional lines—East versus West. In the late 20th century, as new linkages formed between peoples and organizations across continents and as more qualitative demands were made on organizations and states, the industrial systems of management failed. The underlying complexity of different

---

[142] Attributed to Joseph Stalin.

[143] In terms of Command and Control, not equipment.

That he should not be able to command the rain

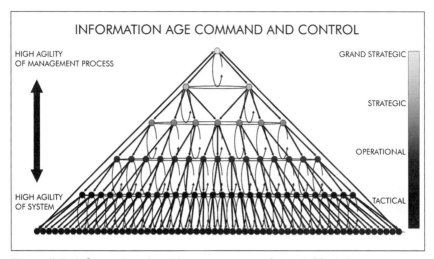

Figure 6.2: Information Age Management applying Ashby's Law

societies, peoples, ethnic groups, companies, and organizations began to be realized and to express themselves adaptively in different systems, not along controlled lines. Increasingly, information management and application had value in itself and, to keep up with the plethora of information now available and to maintain strategic relevance and achieve tactical success, management had to have lateral and vertical agility and interactivity, across and through the different levels as shown in Figure 6.2. "Captains and Corporals" had to be put to better use.

Command and Control in the 21st century requires agile interaction between and across the levels. Thus, while one man's command may well be another's control, the essential component is the interaction of one upon the other. This requires that a command is understood by the controlled and that it is interpreted correctly. On completion of the command or if circumstances change, the command is informed and, where possible, a decision is made or a question raised based upon the

That he should not be able to command the rain

commander's original intent. In this way, Command and Control are made "closed loop" and interactive, between and across the levels. But this is essentially a trust-based and lateral construct: it is neither rule-based nor is it hierarchical or institutional. It involves the commander trusting in his people to "do the right thing" as opposed to "doing things right (by him)" and it requires those he controls to have trust in him. Essentially, this recognizes the fact that modern armed forces are themselves the Complex Adaptive Systems of chapter 2; that, given the requirements for information management and application, they cannot be controlled but may be commanded. The only way that each level can be made to work in an interactive way across and between the levels is to encourage Delegated Autonomous Command—disaggregating command across the different levels and encouraging efficient asynchronous working from which patterns of synchronicity may emerge. And the good commander, as always, needs to then recognize these patterns—indeed "he should not be able to command the rain."

EFFECT OF COMMAND

If one does not achieve some form of Delegated Autonomous Command, then the level at which command is vested becomes increasingly important. The complex battlespace in which armed forces are placed increasingly requires forces to be engaged simultaneously in a range of activities from peace enforcement in one space to peace stabilization in another, and warfighting in yet another. To cope, this "multi-space war" requires a high degree of command fidelity and control agility—it cannot be controlled. And attempts to control this type of battlespace, even if possible, will take an overwhelming preponderance of time and mass to succeed. Control, therefore, is also associated with time and, through time (and the need to exercise control across the different layers) to the technical means of exerting control. The more one wishes to exert control over a particular part of the battlespace, the more time it will take and the greater the bandwidth requirements will be. In simple terms,

> control is a function of rules, time, and bandwidth,[144] whereas command is a function of trusts, fidelity, and agility.

In an open loop organization where there is little or no interaction between the commanded and the controlled, the only way to achieve the aim is by means of securing the bandwidth and mass necessary to buy enough time for the desired effect to be realized. Command is imbalanced by control. Where command and control are interactive, they are more in balance and it is possible to offset requirements for time and bandwidth through fidelity and agility. Control is therefore a function of command as command is of control. Organizations have a choice: if they wish to exert control over the battlespace, as opposed to command, they need to provide the rules and quantitative technological bandwidth necessary. If they wish to command, as opposed to control the battlespace, they need to provide the more qualitative trusts of fidelity and agility in their people. Taken one step further, command is more associated with culture and control with technology; and it is the effect of one upon the other that is key. Command and Control also underpins Transformation, with a widespread recognition that Revolutions in Military Affairs (RMAs) have been brought

---

[144] And bandwidth as provided by communications systems is itself is a function frequency and time. Wider bandwidth systems are provided by SHF (satellite communications), themselves always in finite supply and expensive.

about by technological advances applied by new or emerging cultures,[145] not by technology alone.

U.K. armed forces tend to provide significant Distributed Autonomous Command to their Leading Hands and Corporals. A recent RAND study recognized that command in the U.S. armed forces tended to be vested at the Colonel or Captain (USN) level.[146] Where command is vested and exercised has important implications to the realization of both Effects Basing and NEC/NCW. In Iraq, Bosnia, and the other trouble spots in which the U.S. and the U.K. find themselves fighting alongside each other, both force protection and freedom of movement are important military outcomes. By vesting command at the Corporal level, the U.K. makes the platoon highly interactive both with its immediate command and the environment in which it is placed. By retaining command at a higher level and not similarly disaggregating it, interaction with the environment and immediate commands is limited. Both the U.S. and the U.K. achieve the outcome of delivering both force protection and freedom of movement, admirably and despite difficult conditions, but they do so differently. The U.K. relies upon the Corporal or Leading Hand to make decisions locally, calling on support and "gatting up"[147] as required. Forces are often "light" (soft skinned Landrovers) with suitable back-up on call. U.S. forces, by comparison, tend to be armed permanently

---

[145] "True RMAs tend therefore to bring together a number of technological advances and combine them with broader changes in society and politics, as well as the necessary adaptation in organization and doctrine." Benbow, "The Revolution in Military Affairs."

[146] Anecdotal evidence would tend to confirm this. Certainly I (Atkinson) have seen Leading Hands and Corporals making the type of decisions reserved for senior ratings or junior Lieutenants in the U.S. Navy and Army.

[147] Donning body armor and helmets in place of berets and combat 95 uniform.

Effect of command

and patrol in four to six heavily armored Humvees, rather than on foot. The inputs and outcomes are the same, but the outputs can be very different in terms of men and materiel.

The risks too are different. On the one hand, the U.K. is prepared to trust its people to command appropriately but, in doing so, it potentially places them at greater risk than U.S. personnel. The U.S. appears less prepared to risk Delegated Autonomous Command and so places its trust more in technological control than its people. In isolation, arguably, the equations appear to achieve the same, albeit differently. If one considers, though, that both forces are also dealing with the Complex Adaptive Systems provided by their local operational environment and that a significant part of U.K. force protection is based upon interaction between it and the local people,[148] then the two may provide very different, wider outcomes, such as stabilization versus enforcement. Interaction with the local environment can also provide a type of early warning.[149]

In sum, how and where one vests command, and so controls, influences not just technological requirements and resources but also outputs and outcomes, despite similar inputs.

THE IMPORTANCE OF AGILITY

Differences between the way in which U.S. and U.K. forces aggregate and are aggregated have been used by way of example to show that, even given similar inputs, the outputs may be

---

[148] The Tommy as opposed to the "Bobby on the beat."

[149] Interaction with local people or the lack of it can often be a first indicator or warning to a patrol that things may be amiss, but this does require prior-connection between the different players.

very different, even if the same outcomes are achieved. But a capacity that both the U.S. and the U.K. are looking to engender within their forces is that of agility, an ability of the forces to adapt, to learn and to change to meet the threats that they face. Agility, as we see it, is a network commodity, inherent to a network and the way that it formed and adapted to the circumstances and context in which it first emerged. Successful organizations need to retain this essential network characteristic over time, and preserve (and so protect) it within their way of doing business, the way that they aggregate, command, and control themselves—in effect their "rules," doctrines, and modus operandi. It is here that the British and American structures may also show a marked cultural difference that affects the way both operate and behave.

We have argued that the British tend to engender network agility within the lower echelons of their armed forces, often to overcome structural constraints without which mass would be the only solution. The U.S., by contrast, form their linkages (and hence networks) at higher levels and engender agility at this level and above, not necessarily below. Given their history, since World War II, it is certainly the case that the British have built up a well of experience for dealing with enforcement and stabilization operations based upon the agility and flexibility shown by its lower echelons from the Palestine, Borneo, Malaya, through to Northern Ireland and Afghanistan. To a great extent, it has not had to learn new patterns and ways of doing business from others, since this well of experience has always been at hand and has coped with the forms of warfare with which it has been dealing. A similar reliance and belief in British experience and ways of doing business may have been exhibited during World War II up until D-Day. Initially, at least after El Alamein and the long fight back against the Japanese after the fall of Singapore and against the U-boats in the North Atlantic, the British were probably right to be in their own comfort zone and skeptical of American ideas, views, and doctrines. But it can be argued that this prejudice perhaps persisted too long—showing an inability for some of the more senior structures within the British armed forces to adapt and change to changing circumstances: to show agility.

This was brought to a head in the months and weeks before the breakout from the D-Day beachheads as the British and Americans fought through the "brockage" of Normandy. British forces used a series of tightly controlled engagements to take Caen, absorbing as they did so much of the German counter-offensive. The American forces adopted a more maneuverist approach to swing past German concentrations, using airpower as a force multiplier to offset German mass advantage. The U.S. Army, under command of Eisenhower, thus appeared to adapt to the circumstances and learn more quickly than the British. Similarly, having been ejected from the Far East by the Japanese, the Royal Navy had had to adopt U.S. methods—the Fleet Train, for example—to fight and pervade alongside the U.S. Navy as it won its way back across the vast tracts of the Pacific Ocean. It would appear, therefore, that while the British engendered agility within their lower echelons and relied upon the experience this had gained them with which to fight effectively, their agility at the higher levels may have been somewhat less; perhaps more institutionalized and so formalized than the equivalent U.S. structures and, as part of an enduring establishment, less risk-taking and thus less able to change.

The War on Terror may also exhibit a similar dichotomy in the agility shown between U.K. and U.S. forces. The British entered the War on Terror with a well of experience built up during similar campaigns stretching back over decades and 30 years in Northern Ireland. Up to a point they felt that there was little that the U.S. armed forces could tell them—and up to a point they were right. The Americans entered the War on Terror in response to an attack on the U.S. mainland—not because, hitherto, they had wanted to or because of historical and colonial responsibilities that meant that they had little or no choice. The agility that specialist arms of the U.S. showed in Afghanistan in the orchestrating of an air campaign—sometimes from horseback—and working with disparate tribal warlords to engender an effective coalition with which to defeat the Taliban, should not be underestimated. Neither, too, should the way in which U.S. forces are beginning to learn and adapt to the War in Iraq; listening to their young Captains, Majors, and NGOs and showing a preparedness to adapt and change their methodologies in order to meet the new threat.

The U.S. system, for all its rigidity, and the checks and balances it evolved from the Revolution onwards to protect itself from despotic or tyrannical rule, nevertheless appears to exhibit considerable agility when forced to do so, an ability to form new connections and networks with which to express itself and to transfer its powers effectively. The British system, by contrast, based upon lower level agility and experience in depth has (at least in the past) appeared less risk-taking at the higher levels of command—and thus less agile.

In the final analysis, the U.S. and the U.K. wish to engender agility and an ability to adapt and overcome throughout the structures that define and make up their armed forces. For the British, this may mean creating similar agile network structures within senior joint and MoD commands as exhibited within

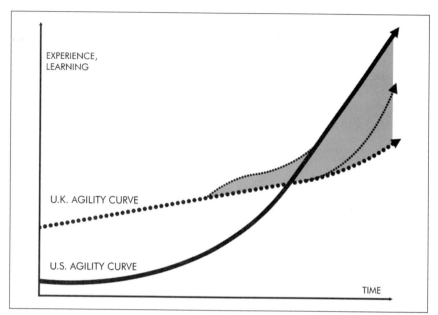

Figure 6.3: Agility Curves

the fighting structures. For the U.S., this may require adopting more networked structures through their lower echelons and delegating command more. For both countries, it will require controlling less and commanding more.

The schematic diagram above (Figure 6.3) suggests that an organization's ability to learn and to apply its experience is a function of its agility over time. The curve below suggests that the U.K. and U.S. "Agility Curves" may be different as a result of the way that their forces and command infrastructures are aggregated. It suggests that the more formal senior organizations of the U.K. armed forces may be less agile at their senior ranks: less able to learn and more willing to apply what has worked in the past, or their own experience, to a problem. The U.S. system, by contrast, may be less agile at the lower echelons and so has less experience to go on, but it is more agile and net-

workable at the senior echelons, where it is prepared to change
and to learn as circumstances demand. Iraq has been a testing
experience for both the British and U.S. armed forces—both
have coped admirably with the different conditions (the U.K.
in the Shia south and the U.S. in the Sunni center and Kurdish
north). But, after a slow start, anecdotal evidence suggests that
U.S. forces are learning fast.

If these assumptions are correct, in time, and despite starting
lower down the curve, history suggests that the U.S. agility
curve will bypass the U.K. one (which is based more upon previous experience). The question as to when and by how much
will be determined by the U.K.'s willingness, need, and ability
to learn from the U.S., and when it commences the process.
Previous experience suggests that this could be a painful experience—the earlier the better to avoid "catch-up." This is
illustrated in Figure 6.3 by two possible options. The first (the
left-hand dotted line) shows the U.K. reacting quickly to the
U.S. increase in agility, with little or no catch-up. The second
(right-hand dotted line) shows a more difficult transition.

CHAPTER 7

BACK TO THE FUTURE

Complexity ➡ Networks ➡ Effects ➡ Agility

In this final chapter, we conclude by discussing the need for a shift towards the creation of informal, adaptive, and complex networks of interaction that will have sufficient agility to match our adversaries. We start by exploring the nature of command in these new circumstances a little further.

BOUNDING COMMAND

Industrial Age command was based upon Directed Control applied rigidly within narrowly defined stovepipes or "institutes." It worked only for as long as other commands were prepared to play by the same rules. As soon as these rules were challenged, control failed and command crumbled. Globalization and the Information Revolution[150] at the end of the 20th century created many goods, in particular the degree of con-

---

[150] In the way in which information became available to all in a similar way that the Industrial Revolution released energy and automotive power to most.

nectedness and interactivity that it achieved between states, peoples, and organizations. Globalization and the Information Revolution therefore brought with them new and more complex forms of aggregation, highly adaptive to their local environment and associated systems. Quite rapidly, older, more linear systems, designed around centralized control of one type or another, began to fail. Most successful states were able to cope with the changes that emerging constructs began to demand from the mid-1970s onward, when most of the old heavy industries and their associated, demarcated practices were swept away. Bankrupted by its failure to keep pace with Western re-armament and to divest itself of highly inefficient practices, the Soviet Union itself failed in 1989. And, as the old linear certainties of the Cold War ended, states formed during this period also began to fail, as did some formed from the collapse of the Soviet Union. Taking a rudimentary and brutal yardstick to the 200-odd states that make up the U.N. in 2004, one could suggest that as few as 50 states[151] exercise power in an accountable and legitimized fashion recognizable to the signatories of Atlantic Charter of 1945. Of the remaining 150, 50 might be considered as failing (in one regard or another), and 50 as failed.

The Information Age also brought with it an illusion or panacea that it might be possible to exercise control from the center after all, that VTC,[152] new information systems, and ever-greater bandwidth and computing power would enable *command* to be *controlled*, and that, somehow, technology could, in itself, create the necessary interaction across the layers to enable *automated control*: that processes could be controlled

---

[151] Most of Europe, North America, and India.

[152] Video-Television-Conferencing.

through automation and it was only a matter of devising yet more capable computers and information systems. This may also represent a deep cultural divide between the U.S. and the U.K. In the U.S., there is a belief that technology can and will provide the answers, whereas in the U.K. there is a higher degree of skepticism, and a belief that culture will overcome the challenges. Both positions are probably right and each colored by experience but both, nevertheless, act as policy drivers within institutions tasked with driving change in both countries. This can cause subtle but nevertheless major differences in policy trajectories. For example, U.S. Transformation creates jointery at the 4- and 5-star level (rather than between and across the different services), further reinforced by a fundamental belief in technological solutions to provide effect. While U.K. forces, jointly aggregated, are looking to create better enabled networks so as to leverage more effect from existing capabilities, both cultural and technological (for example, through the development of common processes and common training). And these differences are further exacerbated by differences in the way the U.K. and the U.S. understand and so exercise Command and Control.

Setting aside these differences for the moment, if it is accepted that "RMAs tend to bring together a number of technological advances and combine them with broader changes in society and politics," then it will be necessary to address and so to adapt cultural "issues of organization and doctrine."[153] As we have seen, key to the delivery of this change will be how forces are aggregated and so commanded and controlled. If it is further accepted that:

---

[153] Benbow, "The Revolution in Military Affairs."

- The behavior of Complex Adaptive Systems cannot be controlled;
- Some form of delegated autonomous control is needed to encourage interactive autonomous behavior from which synchronous patterns may emerge; and
- The creation of effects requires us to achieve improved levels of fidelity and agility across the battlespace,

then a new form of exercising Command and Control (across and between the different levers and levels of power) is required.

Information Age command will require an acceptance that technology can aid command, but cannot dominate it—that despite huge advances in computing power, technology will never be able to replace the essential components of command necessary to deal with a highly complex and adaptive environment; that the essential fidelity across the levers of power and agility between the different levels necessary for Effects Based Operations is provided by command, as balanced and aided by control. Accepting the above, it is possible to consider ways in which Information Age command might be arranged.

Crucially, new patterns of command will need to delegate authority to lower levels of command to encourage self-organization and autonomous/asynchronous patterns of behavior. To achieve this, lower command levels will need to have trust in their commander and confidence in what is expected of and from them. U.K. concepts of Command Intent may provide for this type of delegated authority—with the intentions acting to guide the different communities. Common information and the development of common processes and common training will also help to build such trust. Essentially, this is a bounding process: bounding the different grand to strategic to opera-

Bounding command

tional and tactical levels and levers of power in a way that maintains coherency with Commanders' Intent, through self-synchronization. Bounding is not a predictive or linear process: it involves the commander and those commanded in an inter-active process, whereby the different levels and levers interact with each other laterally to explore their boundaries asynchro-nously and determine gaps and discontinuities. These individuals then have the confidence/trust to either "fill the gap" or to report discontinuities up the chain, synchronously and by default, not by rule. At no stage are the patterns of work controlled more they are bounded within the intent set by the commander: his trust in them and theirs in him. But Com-mand Guidance does not stop with the issuing of Command Intent: through a series of information gathering interactions, the commander provides guidance to his bounds, interactively trusted to fine tune his plan.

As introduced in chapters 2, 3, and 4, this is about the man-agement of Small World Networks or communities of interest in that these networks are scaled and clustered about certain pre-ordained groups with clear tasks. They are not Scale Free Networks, where new nodes are joining continually and clus-ters form naturally about the most attractive and/or connected nodes. Effective communities of interest perform two functions. On the one hand, their clusters are pre-ordained and so are formal, hierarchical, rule-based deposi-tories of power. On the other hand, these clusters act to encourage lateral networks to form about them where power can be distributed through the grid in a bounded or scaled way. If delegated autonomous command is exercised prop-erly, such clusters should form naturally.

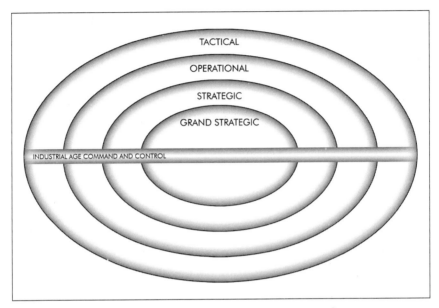

TACTICAL

OPERATIONAL

STRATEGIC

GRAND STRATEGIC

INDUSTRIAL AGE COMMAND AND CONTROL

Figure 7.1: Bounded command applying Communities of Interest

In Figure 7.1, bounded patterns begin to appear surrounding the pre-ordained clusters running through its center. Industrial Age command in effect took a slice through the middle—rigidly controlled from the center within tightly applied (lateral and horizontal) stovepipes with individuals performing in a strictly de-limited, linear, and hierarchical way. Information Age command needs to do things differently if it is to harness the highly efficient and distributive potential of networks necessary in order to deliver effects. Figure 7.1 suggests this type of arrangement: the different grand strategic, strategic, operational, and tactical levels are bounded, not de-limited or controlled. Thus, while pre-ordained clusters run through the middle of each bounded level, command ripples outwards from the center to empower a number of different bounded networks—networks, that themselves will increasingly include nodes, organizations, and people not directly under the commanders' direct command.[154] Power is distributed in a lateral way with each boundary, cluster, and node interacting with the others through to the tactical moment at which one engages with the "other." Technology is used where required, not to replace command but to aid it and to allow for the control of those parts of the battlespace where orders (rules) need to be translated into actions.

STOVEPIPES TO COMMUNITIES

Headquarter Staffs in the late 20th century were based upon constructs modelled first upon Napoleon's staffs, and then as applied by Federal forces during the U.S. Civil War. Essentially, Headquarters were formed into a number of different functional organizations, originally 1 to 5, around specialist staffs.

After the First World War, these constructs[155] were expanded to include a sixth organization—communications—and, following the Second World War, expanded further to include Force Development, Finance and Budgets, and in the 21st century, Experimentation. Each organization was pre-fixed with a letter, so that G indicated Ground, N for Naval, A for Air, and J for Joint: for example, staffs would frequently refer to J4, instead of Logistics. By the late 20th century, too, additional staffs were being placed into the Headquarters, including political and legal advisers (POLADs and LEGADs), often drawn from OGDs and/or non-military staffs.

---

[154] Such as Other Government Departments, NGOs, and Alliance Commands.

[155] 1 for Manpower, 2 for Intelligence, 3 for Operations, 4 for Logistics, and 5 for Planning.

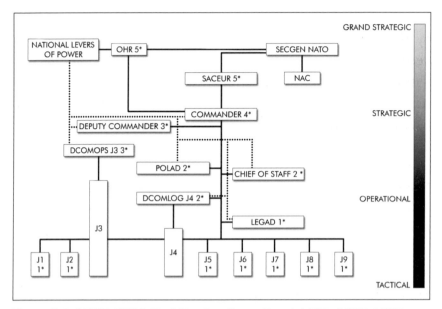

Figure 7.2: NATO SFOR (Stabilization Force, Bosnia) HQ, 1995-1997

The Alliance (NATO) Headquarters construct used by IFOR and SFOR (1995-1999) is presented in Figure 7.2. As can be imagined, the key staffing positions[156] below COMSFOR (a U.S. 4-star general) were fought over fiercely and abrogated as much due to military capability as political will. DCOMSFOR was a Frenchman; DCOMOPS a Briton; Chief of Staff a German; DCOMLOG, U.K. or NL; POLAD, a Dane; and LEGAD an American. Other J function leads were not considered as important and so not allocated the same weighting or attention. Ultimately, SFOR was under the civil lead of the Officer of the High Representative (OHR) in partnership with NATO—SecGen and the North Atlantic Council (NAC) —all as mandated by the U.N. Security Council.

---

[156] D/COMSFOR, Deputy/Commander SFOR; DCOMOPS, Deputy Commander Operations; DCOMLOG, Deputy Commander Logistics.

Not surprisingly, based as it is upon Industrial Age command, by the 21st century this type of headquarters construct had become hopelessly inefficient.[157] Complicated enough on national, let alone alliance lines, the staffs were highly stove-piped and there was little room for individual initiative or lateral interaction between the different staffs. The process was linear. Under the Direction of the Chief of Staff and J5 (Plans), plans would be put forward to the 1-star leads for approval. Plans would then be re-worked by the different staffs before being submitted to the deputy commanders for approval; often this was the first opportunity for the POLAD and LEGAD to be involved. They would then be re-worked before finally being taken forward to the commander for approval. At the same time, in both KFOR[158] and SFOR, SACEUR and Sec-Gen would be working their own plans and applying pressure[159] on COMSFOR to agree these or subsume them into his own planning.

As per Industrial Age production, to provide *quantitative* agility, staffs created many different plans from the same inputs using mass to provide *qualitative choice*. Commands, at whatever level the plans were presented, had to choose one from another. These were then re-worked until a series of approved plans were presented for final selection and amendment. In an alliance headquarters (based upon the consent of all or a majority—one state one vote) this could be a hugely laborious

---

[157] Potts, *The Big Issue*.

[158] Kosovo Force.

[159] This came to a head during the Pristina Airport standoff in 1999 when the British local force commander refused an order by the then SACEUR, General Wesley Clark, to seize the airport from the Russians. The standoff was resolved at the Presidential/Prime Minister level in favor of the local commander.

and manpower intensive linear task. Even minor planning quickly became bogged down in the minutiae of directed control within self-constraining stovepipes. Inevitably, to get things done, the more powerful groups organized themselves about the headquarters on a national or functional basis, often bypassing or even ignoring the different J-staffs. Interaction with other organizations tended to occur at the 2- and 3-star level, through the deputy commanders and the POLAD, further demarcating against the existing stovepipes.

Crucially, planning was undertaken in a "stop-go" way in which the plans themselves were never interactive with each other, other staffs, or with the Commanders' Intent. At a series of planning conferences, commanders were faced with selecting a plan from among a series of options presented to them. Without the strict control of the Chief of Staff, often on a superficial basis, the number of plans could keep growing at each stage and from each new input: an open loop. It was a bit like setting out to buy a car without first identifying a requirement (in terms of seats) or the resources (in terms of funding) available and, not surprisingly, ending up with a list of every car ever produced to chose from.[160]

In an alliance construct, operating in a stabilization environment, where perhaps time is less of an issue, these headquarters arrangements may continue to have some merit. But, in the increasingly connected—multi-space—types of war we are now engaged in, they may no longer be

---

[160] An analogy suggested by Major Andrew Firth (JFHQ, Lead U.K. Plans) during Multinational Experiment 3, Feb 04.

able to cope. Initial attempts to replace the existing stovepipes[161] have, however, not necessarily been successful,
simply replacing one set of "9 stovepipes" with another: sub-
suming some of the old J functions within five new
constructs—aspects of J2 intelligence into Knowledge Management (KM) and Information Superiority (IS); J3 renamed
Ops; J4 renamed Logistics; J5 renamed Plans, leaving only
the rumps of J1 (Manpower) and J7 (Force Development) and
Finance/Budgets and Experimentation remaining.

If we are to move military HQs from the Industrial to the
Information Age and realize Effects Basing and NCW/NEC,
we may need to make some significant cultural changes:

- Create adaptive staffing systems that can deal with
  Complexity:
    - This will require vesting command (Delegated
      Autonomous Command) at appropriate levels, from
      central and single commands to joint staffs (civil and
      military), and from Colonels to Corporals;
    - Moving from ruled (institutional) to trusted (more
      networkable) organizational structures; and
    - Accepting that technology may aid but should not
      dominate command.
- Control less and command more:
    - By bounding the different levels and processes in an
      interactive and inclusive, not exclusive, way; and
    - Through the combined processes of Command

---

[161] As advised by SecDef and endorsed by the Joint Chiefs of Staff in 2003
(following Millennium Challenge 02) to establish "Manning for Regional
Combatant Commanders Standing Joint Force HQ." Including a 10-man IS
team; a 22-man Plans team; a 16-man Operations team; a 6-man KM team
under the direction of a 4-man "Command Group."

> Intent and interactively applied Command Guidance.

- Act more as Communities of Interest:
  - That allow Bounded Networks to form about them across and between the different levels and levers of power;
  - That allow for asynchronous working from which synchronous patterns may emerge; and
  - That move away from stop-go planning towards a more attuned translation of intent and actions into effects.

FROM CONSENT TO CONCESSIVE

The giving of consent within an alliance construct and the consensual way in which plans are put forward for agreement is essentially stop-go. As a process, it does not narrow the product down, qualitatively, but continues to provide quantitative choice. It is a rule- and control-based mechanism in which to exercise power and influence. The point about Bounded Networks is that power is distributed or delegated through them—as per a grid—rather than concentrated within a central organization. And these Bounded Networks cannot be controlled, they must rely upon the confidence and competence of the staff to work autonomously and asynchronously, forming through self-synchronization to report back or take actions within their bounds. And the bounds, in this regard, are not fixed or controlled; they need to adapt as required. Reporting back, too, is not scripted but by default: if discontinuities are found and they cannot be re-connected, individuals can signal their intentions to command along the lines of "I intend to do X at such a time, unless advised otherwise." This allows commands to be informed and to take action asynchronously and as necessary within the time permitted: it is not stop-go and neither does it require the commanders' approval for a variety of different policy suggestions. Command Intent and Command Guidance therefore work both ways and, as interactive processes, they act to build trust and so agility across and between commands, staffs, and practitioners.

The making of consent is a stop-go process[162]—it is by rule and it uses control to exercise command. In an adaptive and complex environment, this type of decisionmaking process buys up valuable time and adds to the risk of failure: the British Expeditionary Force in 1940. A different means of agreeing decisions needs to be developed. This is called *concessive*, as opposed to consensual. Concessive decisionmaking is about trust: trusting in individual staffs and commands to do the right thing and so enabling one or another to lead, as guided by other involved and so pre-connected parties. Ultimately, it should allow command to exercise authority, seamlessly, across services, staffs, and nations. Concessive decisionmaking may be considered as:

> A specific indication of intent based upon the will and authority of an individual entity and/or the whole for the purpose of permitting synchronized combined action by previously bounded, autonomous, and asynchronous parties.

We are often in danger of believing that these types of arrangements are new, but this is not the case. The Battle of Trafalgar was won on the basis of three "general signals," to the second

---

[162] Taken to be "an indication of will between disconnected parties that expresses the common view of the whole for permitting, complying with and so authorising collective, ruled action."

of which ("England Expects...") Admiral Cuthbert Colling-wood, Nelson's second in command, responded "that he wished Nelson would stop signalling, since they all knew well enough what they had to do."[163] The British fleet that fought at Trafalgar was a close-knit, trust-based, highly trained, and experienced network of highly interlinked commands: Nelson's "band of brothers."[164] Communications did not allow for political influence other than the strategic direction given to each Flag and Captain on assuming command. Through this trust-based network, Nelson was able to divide his fleet and, with himself (uniquely for the time) leading on the Victory and Collingwood on the Royal Sovereign, strike the French and Spanish line simultaneously at its center: "crossing the line." The allied French and Spanish fleets, although larger in number and with more powerful warships, did not have the collective experience to exercise concessive disaggregated and asynchronous command. They were controlled from the center, its weakest point and exactly where Nelson chose to strike, with little room for independent, asynchronous command.

By crossing the line, Nelson also brought to bear his tactical advantage: that of better weaponry and targeting skills (British ships trained to fight on the downward swing and engage the smaller area of the hull as opposed to sails and masts that the Spanish and French targeted on the upswing) and striking at the weakest part of a ship, its stem and stern, where the most

---

[163] Warner, "The Life and Letters of Vice-Admiral Lord Collingwood." p. 150.

[164] The trust Nelson established and exploited at Trafalgar is all the more impressive considering that "only 5 of his 25 'ships of the line' at Trafalgar had formed part of the Mediterranean Fleet and only eight of the captains had ever fought a line-of-battleship in a Fleet action. Most of them had never met him before he took over command 3 weeks before Trafalgar, but all knew of his reputation and all were immediately attracted by his charm." Roger, *The Command of the Ocean.* pp. 537-538.

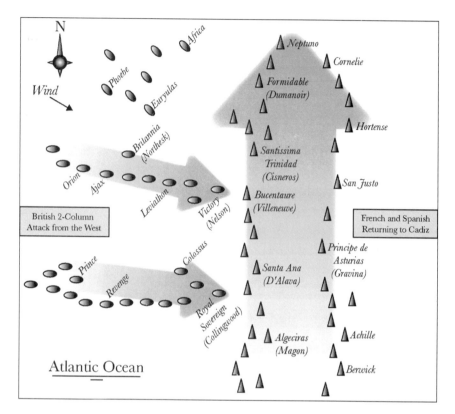

Figure 7.3: The British attack on the Spanish and French fleets

damage could be inflicted. Nelson used his strategic advantage to attack the French and Spanish Fleets at their weakest tactical (ships) and strategic (command) points. "Brilliant and decisive as Trafalgar was, the battle had no immediate impact on the war. Indeed its significance was overshadowed by Napoleon's overwhelming victory over the Austrian and Russian armies at Austerlitz on 2 December."[165] But his victory, while not ending the war, did have strategic impact: it allowed Britain to dominate the oceans for the next 100 years; it enabled the landing of British troops in Portugal in 1808; and it

---

[165] Clayton and Craig, *Trafalgar*. pp. 371-2.

removed any serious threat of invasion. Ultimately, France and Napoleon had to be defeated on land 10 years later, at Waterloo in 1815.

INSTITUTIONAL FRICTION

The Royal Navy failed to learn properly the Nelson lesson, continually applying misguided notions of control as opposed to command that almost lost the Battle of Jutland. Indeed, it is probable that the tactics developed by Nelson or indeed Nelson himself, would not have been acceptable to the Royal Navy from the mid-19th through the mid-20th century.

Taking another example, by the end of the 20th century, the explosion in information systems had begun to challenge the old institutional arrangements by providing an often-dislocated means of aggregation. The investigation into the Columbia Space Shuttle incident (its damage upon takeoff and subsequent disintegration over Texas on its return flight) raised some interesting legal points. Notable amongst these were criticisms of emails and PowerPoint engineering.[166]

Essentially, within the rule-based and hierarchical safety control system, information was being lost. The right information existed, but within the almost tangential network of unofficial emails, exchanged on a trust basis by engineers and scientists working alongside, but outside, the hierarchical control chain. Truths established by NASA's scientific and engineering networks were not getting through to those who needed them, crucially to those who *needed*, even if they did not want, to know.

---

[166] For further discussion, see Edward Tufte's analysis of Boeing slides:
http://www.edwardtufte.com/bboard/q-and-a-fetch-msg?msg_id=0000Rs&topic_id=1&topic=Ask+E.T.

The launch of the Shuttle Columbia on Jan. 16, 2003 at 10:39 EST

Review of Test Data Indicates Conservatism for Tile Penetration

- **The existing SOFI on tile test data used to create Crater was reviewed along with STS-87 Southwest Research data**
  - **Crater overpredicted penetration of tile coating significantly**
    - **Initial penetration to described by normal velocity**
      - Varies with volume/mass of projectile (e.g., 200ft/sec for 3cu. In)
    - **Significant energy is required for the softer SOFI particle to penetrate the relatively hard tile coating**
      - Test results do show that it is possible at sufficient mass and velocity
    - **Conversely, once tile is penetrated SOFI can cause significant damage**
      - Minor variations in total energy (above penetration level) can cause significant tile damage
  - **Flight condition is significantly outside of test database**
    - **Volume of ramp is 1920cu in vs 3 cu in for test**

6

One of the slides presented by the Boeing engineering team while the damaged shuttle was in orbit: the top half appears to indicate minimal risk to the shuttle, however the bottom half reveals that the shuttle may have sustained serious damage and may be in great danger

Moreover, briefs taken by NASA tended to interpret Power-Point presentations as firsthand truths.

Similar examples of this confusion can be seen occurring within the essentially rule-orientated signalling system that has at its core action/information addressees and orders of precedence. By contrast, emails are directed individually, not collectively, cannot be prioritized in terms of precedence, and often bypass legitimate chains of command.

Author Simon Atkinson:

> My Deputy in HMS OCEAN was tasked directly via email by a shore authority to perform certain trials without copying the command or myself. If my Deputy had not raised this email to my attention, he might otherwise have embarked upon a set of trials, which at the time would have had a serious operational impact. The legitimate course of action required the appropriate resources to be requested through command, officially by signal, not unofficial email. Emails and PowerPoint briefs have their legitimate purpose for the exchange of lateral information, but alone, they do not create legitimate action or purpose within a command chain or its associated control systems. The two are not synonymous. Interaction between the two systems is vital.

The Columbia investigation, after the fact, attempted to pin down the rules applying at the time and to distinguish between those who had command from those with control. Within the new information environment, this proved difficult to do. The NASA scientific and engineering community was working legitimately, as was its Command and Control system. The problem was that these two bodies were not interacting. For a combination of reasons, perhaps that the trust-based networks did not trust the NASA hierarchy or that the hierarchy did not permit "frank exchange or interaction" with its scientific community, information was being lost.

What appeared to be missing between NASA and its engineering and scientific communities were the gatekeepers and gamekeepers necessary to "beat the bounds," allowing for the concessive and interactive transfer of commands and truths to and from the battle and rule spaces—the one to guide flows of information, the other to protect its trusts. Ultimately, within NASA, one had a combination of institutional bodies and networked clusters that were themselves failing to interact. Modelled, as it is, upon military lines, this should send a warning signal to those other organizations attempting to combine new practices without understanding the truths and changes necessary to make them work.

TRUST EXCHANGES

To fight effectively, one needs to have trust in one's fellow sailors, soldiers, and airmen to do the right thing. Extending beyond this, one needs trust between one's commanders and, in an alliance or coalition, between one's political leaders and states to engage forces appropriately. Yet, as we have suggested in chapters 5 and 6, to be effective, alliances needs to move from a ruled to more of a trusted state: from a formal organization to more of a Small World Network. Hence, in most recent examples of warfighting, one has tended to see such coalition networks emerging from within a pre-existing alliance. These coalition networks have tended to form the scaled hub of a wider alliance or coalition construct responsible for prosecuting the war and from which key coalition/alliance assets are commanded. The issue, ultimately, comes down to trust and how trust may be developed over time and so exchanged between forces of different nationalities when circumstances require. In Afghanistan, Iraq, and the Global War on Terrorism, these Small World coalition networks have consisted of three countries: the U.S. (as lead), Australia, and the U.K. Exchanges between these three states have been frank and direct; lessons have been learned and mistakes made, but trusts have been established and renewed. It is too late to start developing trusts in the face of battle, when one has to believe and to trust already in one's fellow combatants and commanders to be effective. The question then becomes how to engender such trusts in peacetime so as to be effective in wartime?

The basis of this book is that we are all connected and interconnected in some way: the rule of six degrees referred to in chapter 4, "no man is an island." From the point of view of Game Theory (for example in economics), the question is: how does cooperation (trust) emerge from a set of essentially selfish players? In some cases, a "defector" group can "cheat" by living on the cooperation benefit provided by a cooperating group.[167], [168] We call this phenomenon *free riding*. In a military sense, free riding may refer to a state or organization that enjoys benefiting from international defense, without actually contributing fully or at all to it. States, like individuals, face a temptation to cheat, to save their people and dollars by not contributing, while enjoying all of the benefits.

As we have seen in the recent past, one solution is for a small group of nations to act in such a way as to encourage other states to contribute more—by transforming and modernizing—and punishing those who do not, for example by denying them key commands or intelligence access. But this type of behavior does not engender trusts between states and tends towards the combative: you do that and I will veto this. Moreover, it does not create the necessary linkages that will engender trusts between service people of differing nationalities and their multinational commands.

---

[167] Novak and May, "Evolutionary Games and Spatial Chaos." pp. 826-829.

[168] Doebeli et al., "The Evolutionary Origin." pp. 859-862.

Trust exchanges

Tad Hogg, Kay-Yut Chen, and Raymond Beausoli of Hewlett Packard have examined the phenomenon of free riding with regard to public goods and have considered the case where, if a player decides to cheat, the influence of this on the final outcome of the game is revealed to him. As a result, he does not play his hand in isolation or as a one-off move with no immediate consequence, but as part of an interactive sequence with other players. In such a gaming sequence, the decision by one alliance nation to play their hand in a certain way would be immediately noticeable to the rest of the alliance, as would the potential results of such a decision. The consequences might remain the same, but other alliance partners would be aware of the willingness to cooperate, or its limits, in order to adjust their own strategy accordingly.

Alliance constructs, such as NATO, have tended in the past to position their strategies on a non-interactive basis, and played their votes in isolation (and own national interests). A more interactive voting or gaming mechanism, within an alliance, might deter free riding while giving due warning of potential outcomes, if cooperation and some form of consensus is not achieved. This would help the transition from the stop-go of consent to the smoother interaction of concessive decisionmaking. And, at its heart, it would develop trust-based constructs for cooperation. This type of interaction between staffs is essential if we are to move from (effectively) the linear planning process as practiced currently to some form of Effects Based Planning (as described in chapter 6).

Fighting in a tight-knit, Small World Network, one has no need to create interaction; it is all too obvious in the first place. Each serviceman has to do his duty at one time or another to protect and preserve the rest. No one likes to be that lone man on

Trust exchanges

point, but he has to be trusted to do the job and trust in his colleagues to support him, if the need arises. But beyond this and across coalition commands, service personnel like to think that it is not just them out in front, but that their allies and coalition partners are also sharing some of the burden: "it is not just me." There are two ways of achieving this: one is to move towards some form of integration, where units from different nations merge to become indistinguishable, one from the other, so as to form a seamless whole; and the other is to achieve a degree of interaction between the forces, such that the risks and burdens are shared equitably between the forces, although they fight alongside each other. Each form has its advantages and disadvantages but each form—interactive or integrated—is essentially a network construct. As an interactive coalition partner, depending on scale, one would act more as a node in a Small World Network; whereas, as an integrated entity one would more normally be the cluster or hub at its heart. Within a small world coalition, one would see command structures and certain high-value, low-demand integrated assets forming within the cluster or hub, surrounded by interactive low-value, high-demand nodes. Assembled in such a networked way, a coalition might become more than just a sum of its parts with its effectiveness based upon common trusts, not rules.

FINAL THOUGHTS

The Peace of Westphalia (1648) was significant in many ways. Not only did it bound the characteristics and behavior of the state system, but it also set in motion a very different philosophy and way of thinking. On the one hand, Cardinal Richlieu fought against the Hapsburgs both to challenge the authority of Rome and to ensure a weak central Europe, constrained by the rules of peace. On the other hand, the northern, largely Protestant states were freed by the same rules to pursue arguably their own and more outward looking (international) philosophy, as expressed in the U.K. following its coincident Civil Wars (1639-1651) through John Locke (1632-1704) and Edmund Burke (1729-1797) and finding expression in the American Revolution. These different philosophies resonate to this day, with France perhaps wishing to preserve its strong centrist position and the U.K. wishing to maintain its more international, less ruled, and more flexible position outside the Euro. We may be seeing a reaffirmation of the underlying differences between an essentially linear, rule-based construct that attempts to control peace along the lines of the old centralized Soviet system and a more trust-based, complex construct that seeks adaptive interaction between different systems and commands, based upon interchange and the exchange of peace for goods.[169] In isolation, rule-based constructs may be condemned to failure. Fixed rules, like walls,[170] tend to fail over time.

International Law is not new: it traces its way through Francisco de Vitoria (1492-1546, considered by many to be the father of International Law), Hugo Grotius (1583-1645), Eméric Crucé (1590-1648), and specifically the arrangements between states concluded by the Peace of Westphalia in 1648 (largely influenced by Crucé's ideas). The international legal system arising from the 1945 Atlantic Charter had, at its core, states. States were presumed equal within the U.N. and to be equably operable on a consent basis when it came to the application and enforcement of international treaties and acts.

---

[169] Where goods may be security, laws and good governance as much as services, products, and trade.

[170] For example the Maginot, Berlin, or the Israeli "Peace" Walls.

Final thoughts

Without the means of enforcing its authority, the U.N. had to rely largely on states to achieve the just conditions necessary, *in bello*. In the bipolar politics of the Cold War, adjudicated after the Korean War through the U.N., these applications broadly worked. However, as the essentially state construct of the old Soviet Empire collapsed after the Cold War and new emergent states took shape, the conditions required by International Law could no longer be met in full or in part. Persons and groupings without states took on states, and states took on their people in a complicated realignment of old religious, ethnic, and tribal boundaries,[171] often linked through crime. A new vacuum as pernicious as that existing in the early 17th century had emerged, except this time existing beyond the writ of International Law. And this vacuum was put in stark contrast by 9/11, the behavior of the Taliban in Afghanistan in support of al-Qaeda, and by the prolonged failure of the U.N. to enforce its writ over Iraq.

International Law is unbounded, unconnected, and open loop. It applies coherently only to a minority of states and persons and is concentrated upon *Jus ad Bellum* as opposed to *Jus in Bello* and *Jus post Bellum*. In addition, it has no independent means for enforcing its will. For this it must rely upon states. As epitomized by the U.N., International Law is based upon equability between states that in practice has never existed and that is making it ever harder to arrive at a consensual position. Ultimately, International Law appears biased against the state system, and worse, those "applicable states" more likely to uphold and honor its directives. In an increasingly connected and interlinked world, globalization requires International Law

---

[171] In Somalia, Liberia, Sierra-Leone, Zimbabwe, Yemen, Afghanistan, Kuwait, Saudi Arabia, Columbia, Peru, Haiti, Bosnia, Serbia, Croatia, Kosovo, Macedonia, and Albania, among many others.

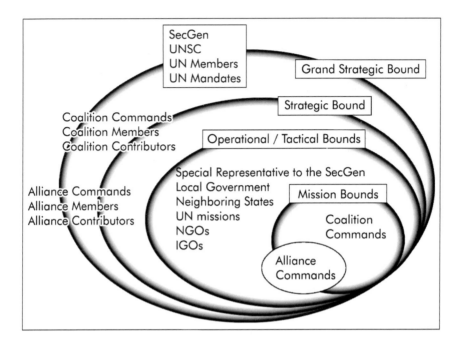

Figure 7.4: Bounding the Future International Environment

to be similarly connected—responsive and adaptive to the many complex systems (states, organizations, or individuals) it is required to interact with, not rule.

Globalization is challenging the way we think and the way we interact across continents, let alone islands. And in this world, no man is an island. We are no longer isolated from our other man as we were before and this new linkage and connectedness brings with it new responsibilities and rights, including a recognition that both war and peace are now "joined permanently" as are prevention and pre-emption— we will have little or no warning. Thus, our future peace will be based upon an understanding of the complex and adaptive systems in which we work; how they interact and

Final thoughts

connect, and how we interchange with them. This will require technological advances, led[172] by cultural change, and for us to understand the "knowledge of causes, and secret motions of things; and the enlarging of the bounds of human empire, to the effecting of all things possible."[173]

---

[172] As the Prime Minister, Tony Blair, stated at his Sedgefield Constituency on 5 March 2004: "Ultimately, *leadership is about deciding.* And my judgement then and now is that the risk of this new global terrorism and its *interaction* with *states* or *organisations* or *individuals* proliferating WMD is one I simply am not prepared to run."

[173] Bacon, *New Atlantis.*

ABOUT THE AUTHORS

SIMON REAY ATKINSON

Simon Reay Atkinson joined the Royal Navy in 1979. After training as an electrical and systems engineer and gaining his first degree, he served in the Falklands, the Gulf during the mine war; then, after the first Iraq war, he served in Bosnia (with the British Army), Sierra Leone, and Nicaragua. Responsible, as the first operational Systems Engineering Officer, for taking HMS OCEAN (the U.K.'s newest and largest (helicopter) carrier) from build to full operational status, he may be considered a specialist amphibious officer. Subsequently, he took an MPhil in International Relations at St. Catharine's College, Cambridge, before working on the New Chapter of the Strategic Defence Review after 9/11 and leading U.K. Force Development work on Networks, Effects Basing, and transformation. He has recently completed a tour to Washington, as the Chief of Defence Staffs' "directed telescope" in the U.S. on Afghanistan, Iraq, and the Global War on Terrorism. He is an active committee member of the Naval Review and has written widely for the review and other professional publications.

JAMES MOFFAT

Jim Moffat is a Senior Fellow of the Defence Science and Technology Laboratory, U.K., a Fellow of the Operational Research Society, a Fellow of the Institute of Mathematics and its Applications, and a visiting Professor at Cranfield University, U.K. He was awarded the President's medal of the Operational Research Society in the year 2000. He holds a first class honors degree and a Ph.D. in Mathematics, and was awarded the Napier medal in Mathematics by Edinburgh University. He has worked for the past 30 years or so on defense-related operational analysis problems, and aerospace technology research. His current research interests are in building tools, models, and theories that capture the key effects of human decisionmaking and other aspects of Information Age conflict. He has published extensively in the peer reviewed open literature. His most recent works include the books *Command and Control in the Information Age: Representing its Impact* (The Stationery Office, London, U.K., 2002) and *Complexity Theory and Network Centric Warfare* (published by CCRP, DoD, U.S.).

BIBLIOGRAPHY

Albert, Reka and Albert-László Barabási. "Statistical Mechanics of Complex Networks." *Reviews of Modern Physics.* Vol 74. Jan 2002.

Alberts, David and Richard Hayes. *Power to the Edge.* Washington DC, USA: CCRP Publication Series. 2003.

Alberts, David, John Garstka, and Frederick Stein. Network Centric Warfare: Developing and Leveraging Information Superiority. Washington, DC, USA: CCRP Publication Series. 1999.

Alberts, David, John Garstka, Richard Hayes, and David Signori. *Understanding Information Age Warfare.* Washington, DC, USA: CCRP Publication Series. 2001.

Alberts, David, Richard Hayes, Daniel Maxwell, Dennis Leedom, and John Kirzl. *Code of Best Practice for Experimentation.* Washington, DC, USA: CCRP Publication Series. 2003.

AP 3003. *A Brief History of the Royal Air Force.* HMSO. 2004.

Bacon, Francis. *New Atlantis.* 1626. http://oregonstate.edu/instruct/phl302/texts/bacon/atlantis.html (May 2005)

Beer, Stafford. *The Heart of Enterprise.* New York, NY, USA: Wiley. 1979.

Beevor, Anthony. *Berlin.* New York, NY, USA: Penguin Books. 2002.

Benbow, Tim. "The Revolution in Military Affairs." Collected Papers. Dstl Unpublished Report. May 2002.

Brook, Peter and Rob Stevens. "NEC: the implications for acquisition." *Journal of Defence Science*. Vol 8 No 3. Sept 2003.

Brooks, Michael. "Dangerous Liaison." *New Scientist*. 16 Aug 2003.

CIO enterprise magazine. April 15, 1998. http://www.cio.com/archive/ 041598/index.html (May 2005)

Clayton, Tim and Phil Craig. *Trafalgar*. London, UK: Hodder and Stoughton. 2004.

Coase, Ronald. "The Nature of the Firm: Influence." Williamson and Winter. *The Nature of the Firm: Origins, Evolution, and Development*. New York, NY, USA: Oxford University Press. 1991.

Cohen, Eliot. *Supreme Command*. New York, NY, USA: The Free Press. 2002.

Cover, Thomas and Joy Thomas. *Elements of Information Theory*. New York, NY, USA: Wiley. 1991.

Disraeli, Prime Minister Benjamin, speech in Edinburgh, Oct 1868.

Doebeli, Michael, Christoph Hauert, and Timothy Killingback. "The Evolutionary Origin of Co-operators and Defectors." *Science*. Vol 306. 2004.

Gabriel, Yiannis, Stephen Fineman, and David Sims. *Organizing and Organizations*. 2nd ed. London, UK: SAGE Publications. 2000.

Gardner, W.J.R.. *Decoding History: the Battle of the Atlantic and Ultra*. New York, NY, USA: Macmillan. 1999.

Gleick, James. *Chaos: Making a New Science*. London, UK: Vintage Books, Random House. 1998.

Ho, Joshua. "The Advent of a New Way of War: Theory and Practice of Effects Based Operations." *Working Paper*. Institute of Defence and Strategic Studies. Singapore. Dec 2003.

Ignatieff, Michael. *Empire Lite*. New York, NY, USA: Vintage. 2003.

Janis, Irving and Leon Mann. *Decision-Making: A Psychological Analysis of Conflict, Choice, and Commitment*. New York, NY, USA: Free Press. 1977.

Jenkins, Roy. *Churchill*. New York, NY, USA: Macmillan. 2001.

Kirkwood, A. "Why do we worry when scientists say there is no risk?" *Disaster Prevention and Management, An International Journal*. Vol 3(2). 1994.

May, Robert. *Simple Mathematical Models with Very Complicated Dynamics*. London, UK: Nature. Vol 261. 1976.

McCann, Carol and Ross Pigeau. "Clarifying the Concepts of Command and Control." *Canadian Military Journal*. Vol 3 No 1. 2002.

Milgram, Stanley. "The Small World Problem." *Psychology Today*. 2. 1967.

Moffat, James. *Command and Control in the Information Age: Representing its Impact*. London, UK: The Stationery Office. 2002.

Moffat, James. *Complexity Theory and Network Centric Warfare*. Washington DC, USA: CCRP Publication Series. 2003.

Neubert, Ralf, Otmar Gorlitz, and Tobias Teich. "Automated Negotiations of Supply Contracts for Flexible Production Systems." *International Journal of Production Economics*. 89. 2004.

Novak, Martin and Robert May. "Evolutionary Games and Spatial Chaos." *Nature*. Vol 359. Oct 29, 1992.

Orwell, George. "The Lion and the Unicorn: Socialism and the English Genius." London, UK: Secker & Warburg. 1941.

Orwell, George. *Nineteen Eighty-Four*. New York, NY, USA: Signet Books. 1949.

Perry, Walter and James Moffat. *Information Sharing Among Military Headquarters: The Effects on Decisionmaking.* CA, USA: RAND. 2004.

Perry, Walter, David Signori, and John Boon. *Exploring Information Superiority.* National Defense Research Institute, CA, USA: RAND. 2004.

Potts, David. The Big Issue: Command and Combat in the Information Age. *The Occasional.* No. 45. Reprinted by Washington, DC, USA: CCRP Publication Series. 2003.

Roger, N.A.M. *The Command of the Ocean.* New York, NY, USA: W.W. Norton. 2005.

Sayigh, Yezid. "The Cambridge Security." *Seminar Record.* 30-31 July 2004.

Shannon, Claude. "A Mathematical Theory of Communication." *Bell System Technical Journal.* Vol 27. 1948.

Showell, J. Fuehrer Conferences on Naval Affairs. London, UK: Greenhill Books. 2005.

Smith, Edward. *Effects Based Operations.* Washington, DC, USA: CCRP Publication Series. 2002.

Tuchman, Barbara. *The Guns of August.* New York, NY, USA: Ballantine Books. 1994.

UK Ministry of Defence Paper. DG INFO/11/5/6/2/1 (CBM). "Agile Command Capability." Jan 2003.

Ullman, Harlan and James Wade. *Shock and Awe: Achieving Rapid Dominance.* Washington, DC, USA: CCRP Publication Series. 1996.

Van der Vat, Dan. *Standard of Power.* London, UK: Hutchinson. 2000.

Verrall, N. "Exploring the Human Aspects of Information Management in the NEC Environment." *Unclassified Report*. Defence Science and Technology Laboratory. Ministry of Defence, UK. July 2004.

Volkan, Vamik. *The Need to have Enemies and Allies*. Nortvale, NJ, USA: Jason Aronson. 1988.

Warner, Oliver. "The Life and Letters of Vice-Admiral Lord Collingwood." *OUP.* 1968.

Watts, Duncan. *Small Worlds*. Princeton, NJ, USA: Princeton University Press. 1999.

Watts, Duncan. Santa Fe Working Paper 00-12-062. NM, USA: Santa Fe Institute. 2000.

Weinberg, Gerhard. *A World at Arms*. Cambridge, UK, New York: Cambridge University Press. 1994.

Willard, Vice Admiral Robert F., US Navy. *Proceedings*. October 2002.

Winterbotham, F.W. *The Ultra Secret*. London, UK: Weidenfeld and Nicolson. 1974.

Zhu, Fang. *Gun Barrel Politics*. Boulder, CO, USA: Westview Press. 1998.

INDEX

A

agile organization 118

agility 4, 93, 116, 118–119, 126–128, 131, 157, 164–167, 169, 172, 181

Ashby's Law of Requisite Variety 126, 130, 156

automated control 170

average path length 46–47, 50, 132, 134

B

Benard cells 25–27

Bose-Einstein condensation 112, 114

Bose-Einstein distribution 114

bounded networks 174, 180

bounding 173

C

chaotic system 26

closed loop 160

closed system 24, 32

cluster 6, 8, 30, 66, 109, 111–112, 114, 136, 173–174

clustering coefficient 45, 47, 50, 67, 100, 132, 134

coevolution 28–29, 31–33, 36, 40, 42, 50, 131–132

coevolve 28, 42

collectivist dynamics 37, 40, 132

command 60, 63, 92–93, 125, 137, 150, 152, 161, 169

command and control 152–153, 156, 159–161, 171–172, 187

E

F

G

Catalog of CCRP Publications

(* denotes a title no longer available in print)

Coalition Command and Control*
(Maurer, 1994)

Peace operations differ in significant ways from traditional combat missions. As a result of these unique
characteristics, command arrangements become far
more complex. The stress on command and control
arrangements and systems is further exacerbated by
the mission's increased political sensitivity.

The Mesh and the Net
(Libicki, 1994)

Considers the continuous revolution in information
technology as it can be applied to warfare in terms
of capturing more information (mesh) and how people and their machines can be connected (net).

Command Arrangements for
Peace Operations
(Alberts & Hayes, 1995)

By almost any measure, the U.S. experience shows
that traditional C2 concepts, approaches, and doctrine are not particularly well suited for peace
operations. This book (1) explores the reasons for
this, (2) examines alternative command arrangement
approaches, and (3) describes the attributes of effective command arrangements.

Standards: The Rough Road to the Common Byte
(Libicki, 1995)

The inability of computers to "talk" to one another is a major problem, especially for today's high technology military forces. This study by the Center for Advanced Command Concepts and Technology looks at the growing but confusing body of information technology standards. Among other problems, it discovers a persistent divergence between the perspectives of the commercial user and those of the government.

What Is Information Warfare?*
(Libicki, 1995)

Is Information Warfare a nascent, perhaps embryonic art, or simply the newest version of a time-honored feature of warfare? Is it a new form of conflict that owes its existence to the burgeoning global information infrastructure, or an old one whose origin lies in the wetware of the human brain but has been given new life by the Information Age? Is it a unified field or opportunistic assemblage?

Operations Other Than War*
(Alberts & Hayes, 1995)

This report documents the fourth in a series of workshops and roundtables organized by the INSS Center for Advanced Concepts and Technology (ACT). The workshop sought insights into the process of determining what technologies are required for OOTW. The group also examined the complexities of introducing relevant technologies and discussed general and specific OOTW technologies and devices.

Dominant Battlespace Knowledge*
(Johnson & Libicki, 1996)

The papers collected here address the most critical aspects of that problem—to wit: If the United States develops the means to acquire dominant battlespace knowledge, how might that affect the way it goes to war, the circumstances under which force can and will be used, the purposes for its employment, and the resulting alterations of the global geomilitary environment?

Interagency and Political-Military Dimensions of Peace Operations: Haiti - A Case Study
(Hayes & Wheatley, 1996)

This report documents the fifth in a series of workshops and roundtables organized by the INSS Center for Advanced Concepts and Technology (ACT). Widely regarded as an operation that "went right," Haiti offered an opportunity to explore interagency relations in an operation close to home that had high visibility and a greater degree of interagency civilian-military coordination and planning than the other operations examined to date.

The Unintended Consequences of the Information Age*
(Alberts, 1996)

The purpose of this analysis is to identify a strategy for introducing and using Information Age technologies that accomplishes two things: first, the identification and avoidance of adverse unintended consequences associated with the introduction and utilization of information technologies; and second, the ability to recognize and capitalize on unexpected opportunities.

Joint Training for Information Managers*
(Maxwell, 1996)

This book proposes new ideas about joint training for information managers over Command, Control, Communications, Computers, and Intelligence (C4I) tactical and strategic levels. It suggests a substantially new way to approach the training of future communicators, grounding its argument in the realities of the fast-moving C4I technology.

Defensive Information Warfare*
(Alberts, 1996)

This overview of defensive information warfare is the result of an effort, undertaken at the request of the Deputy Secretary of Defense, to provide background material to participants in a series of interagency meetings to explore the nature of the problem and to identify areas of potential collaboration.

Command, Control, and the Common Defense
(Allard, 1996)

The author provides an unparalleled basis for assessing where we are and were we must go if we are to solve the joint and combined command and control challenges facing the U.S. military as it transitions into the 21st century.

Shock & Awe:
Achieving Rapid Dominance*
(Ullman & Wade, 1996)

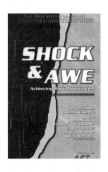

The purpose of this book is to explore alternative concepts for structuring mission capability packages around which future U. S. military forces might be configured.

Information Age Anthology:
Volume I*
(Alberts & Papp, 1997)

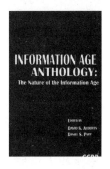

In this first volume, we will examine some of the broader issues of the Information Age: what the Information Age is; how it affects commerce, business, and service; what it means for the government and the military; and how it affects international actors and the international system.

Complexity, Global Politics,
and National Security*
(Alberts & Czerwinski, 1997)

The charge given by the President of the National Defense University and RAND leadership was three-fold: (1) push the envelope; (2) emphasize the policy and strategic dimensions of national defense with the implications for complexity theory; and (3) get the best talent available in academe.

Target Bosnia: Integrating Information Activities in Peace Operations*
(Siegel, 1998)

This book examines the place of PI and PSYOP in peace operations through the prism of NATO operations in Bosnia-Herzegovina.

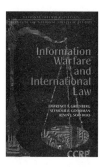

Coping with the Bounds
(Czerwinski, 1998)

The theme of this work is that conventional, or linear, analysis alone is not sufficient to cope with today's and tomorrow's problems, just as it was not capable of solving yesterday's. Its aim is to convince us to augment our efforts with nonlinear insights, and its hope is to provide a basic understanding of what that involves.

Information Warfare and International Law*
(Greenberg, Goodman, & Soo Hoo, 1998)

The authors, members of the Project on Information Technology and International Security at Stanford University's Center for International Security and Arms Control, have surfaced and explored some profound issues that will shape the legal context within which information warfare may be waged and national information power exerted in the coming years.

Lessons From Bosnia:
The IFOR Experience*
(Wentz, 1998)

This book tells the story of the challenges faced and innovative actions taken by NATO and U.S. personnel to ensure that IFOR and Operation Joint Endeavor were military successes. A coherent C4ISR lessons learned story has been pieced together from firsthand experiences, interviews of key personnel, focused research, and analysis of lessons learned reports provided to the National Defense University team.

Doing Windows: Non-Traditional
Military Responses to Complex
Emergencies
(Hayes & Sands, 1999)

This book provides the final results of a project sponsored by the Joint Warfare Analysis Center. Our primary objective in this project was to examine how military operations can support the long-term objective of achieving civil stability and durable peace in states embroiled in complex emergencies.

Network Centric Warfare
(Alberts, Garstka, & Stein, 1999)

It is hoped that this book will contribute to the preparations for NCW in two ways. First, by articulating the nature of the characteristics of Network Centric Warfare. Second, by suggesting a process for developing mission capability packages designed to transform NCW concepts into operational capabilities.

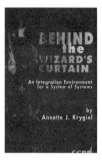

Behind the Wizard's Curtain
(Krygiel, 1999)

There is still much to do and more to learn and understand about developing and fielding an effective and durable infostructure as a foundation for the 21st century. Without successfully fielding systems of systems, we will not be able to implement emerging concepts in adaptive and agile command and control, nor will we reap the potential benefits of Network Centric Warfare.

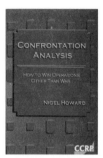

Confrontation Analysis: How to Win Operations Other Than War
(Howard, 1999)

A peace operations campaign (or operation other than war) should be seen as a linked sequence of confrontations, in contrast to a traditional, warfighting campaign, which is a linked sequence of battles. The objective in each confrontation is to bring about certain "compliant" behavior on the part of other parties, until in the end the campaign objective is reached. This is a state of sufficient compliance to enable the military to leave the theater.

Information Campaigns for Peace Operations
(Avruch, Narel, & Siegel, 2000)

In its broadest sense, this report asks whether the notion of struggles for control over information identifiable in situations of conflict also has relevance for situations of third-party conflict management—for peace operations.

Information Age Anthology: Volume II*
(Alberts & Papp, 2000)

Is the Information Age bringing with it new challenges and threats, and if so, what are they? What sorts of dangers will these challenges and threats present? From where will they (and do they) come? Is information warfare a reality? This publication, Volume II of the Information Age Anthology, explores these questions and provides preliminary answers to some of them.

Information Age Anthology: Volume III*
(Alberts & Papp, 2001)

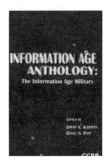

In what ways will wars and the military that fight them be different in the Information Age than in earlier ages? What will this mean for the U.S. military? In this third volume of the Information Age Anthology, we turn finally to the task of exploring answers to these simply stated, but vexing questions that provided the impetus for the first two volumes of the Information Age Anthology.

Understanding Information Age Warfare
(Alberts, Garstka, Hayes, & Signori, 2001)

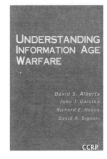

This book presents an alternative to the deterministic and linear strategies of the planning modernization that are now an artifact of the Industrial Age. The approach being advocated here begins with the premise that adaptation to the Information Age centers around the ability of an organization or an individual to utilize information.

Information Age Transformation
(Alberts, 2002)

This book is the first in a new series of CCRP books that will focus on the Information Age transformation of the Department of Defense. Accordingly, it deals with the issues associated with a very large governmental institution, a set of formidable impediments, both internal and external, and the nature of the changes being brought about by Information Age concepts and technologies.

Code of Best Practice for Experimentation
(CCRP, 2002)

Experimentation is the lynch pin in the DoD's strategy for transformation. Without a properly focused, well-balanced, rigorously designed, and expertly conducted program of experimentation, the DoD will not be able to take full advantage of the opportunities that Information Age concepts and technologies offer.

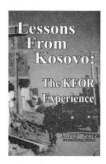

Lessons From Kosovo: The KFOR Experience
(Wentz, 2002)

Kosovo offered another unique opportunity for CCRP to conduct additional coalition C4ISR-focused research in the areas of coalition command and control, civil-military cooperation, information assurance, C4ISR interoperability, and information operations.

NATO Code of Best Practice for C2 Assessment
(2002)

To the extent that they can be achieved, significantly reduced levels of fog and friction offer an opportunity for the military to develop new concepts of operations, new organisational forms, and new approaches to command and control, as well as to the processes that support it. Analysts will be increasingly called upon to work in this new conceptual dimension in order to examine the impact of new information-related capabilities coupled with new ways of organising and operating.

Effects Based Operations
(Smith, 2003)

This third book of the Information Age Transformation Series speaks directly to what we are trying to accomplish on the "fields of battle" and argues for changes in the way we decide what effects we want to achieve and what means we will use to achieve them.

The Big Issue
(Potts, 2003)

This Occasional considers command and combat in the Information Age. It is an issue that takes us into the realms of the unknown. Defence thinkers everywhere are searching forward for the science and alchemy that will deliver operational success.

Power to the Edge:
Command...Control... in the
Information Age
(Alberts & Hayes, 2003)

Power to the Edge articulates the principles being used to provide the ubiquitous, secure, wideband network that people will trust and use, populate with high quality information, and use to develop shared awareness, collaborate effectively, and synchronize their actions.

Complexity Theory
and Network Centric Warfare
(Moffat, 2003)

Professor Moffat articulates the mathematical models and equations that clearly demonstrate the relationship between warfare and the emergent behaviour of complex natural systems, as well as a means to calculate and assess the likely outcomes.

Campaigns of Experimentation:
Pathways to Innovation and Transformation
(Alberts & Hayes, 2005)

In this follow-on to the Code of Best Practice for Experimentation, the concept of a campaign of experimentation is explored in detail. Key issues of discussion include planning, execution, achieving synergy, and avoiding common errors and pitfalls.

Somalia Operations: Lessons Learned (Allard, 2005)

Originally published by NDU in 1995, this book is Colonel Allard's examination of the challenges and the successes of the U.S. peacekeeping mission to Somalia in 1992-1994. Key topics include planning, deployment, conduct of operations, and support.